OVERCOMING HINDRANCES TO YOUR CALLING

HIRAM NJOROGE

UrbanPress
PUBLISHING YOUR DREAMS

Overcoming Hindrances to Your Calling
by Hiram Njoroge
Copyright ©2025 Hiram Njoroge

ISBN 978-1-63360-335-6

Unless otherwise noted, all scripture quotations are taken from the New King James Version®. Copyright © 1982 by Thomas Nelson. Used by permission. All rights reserved.

Scripture notations marked NIV are taken from THE HOLY BIBLE, NEW INTERNATIONAL VERSION®, NIV® Copyright © 1973, 1978, 1984, 2011 by Biblica, Inc.® Used by permission. All rights reserved worldwide.

For Worldwide Distribution
Printed in the U.S.A.

Urban Press
PO Box 5044
Williamsburg, VA 23188-5200
757.808.5776
www.urbanpress.us

CONTENTS

INTRODUCTION

When I wrote my first book, *God's Plan for Your Life Is in His Book*, I wanted to help people uncover and live out the destiny that God has already recorded for them in His Word. I preached those messages to the congregation of Truth Bible Church, the fellowship my wife and I planted in Tucson, Arizona. I shared what the Lord had taught me: that every believer's life has already been written by God, and our role is to discover, embrace, and live out what is in His book.

In *God's Plan*, I taught that God's Word contains not only promises and commandments but also the blueprints of our individual lives—where we are to go, what we are to do, and how we are to be victorious. The book emphasized themes such as dominion, identity in Christ, and the importance of walking in obedience. I explained how Scripture is not just a general record of God's work with humanity but a personal manual revealing God's specific plan for each of us. My personal testimony, along with biblical examples of figures like John the Baptist and Jesus, helped ground the teaching in practical faith. The message was clear: we were born to walk in purpose, reign in life, and live in the confidence of God's promises.

That first book laid the foundation. This second book—what you are now holding—builds upon that message. If *God's Plan* was about discovering God's plan, *Overcoming Hindrances to Your Calling: Living in the Fullness of God's Plan for Your Life* is about identifying and overcoming the hindrances that keep us from fulfilling that plan.

Too many believers know there is a plan for their lives, yet still live in frustration, defeat, or confusion. Why? Because something—often multiple things—is standing in the way. Whether it's complacency, fear, convenience, or a divided heart, these internal obstacles are often more limiting than any external challenge we may face. That's why I wrote this book: to expose the common hindrances that block our progress and to point the way forward in faith, action, and wholehearted devotion.

Why A Second Book?

When I began teaching on the hindrances to God's plan, I could feel the room shift. People were leaning in. They knew they were called. They knew what God had promised. They knew what they believed. But they also knew something was not connecting in their everyday lives. They weren't seeing the fulfillment they expected. That's when I realized that God's people don't just need inspiration—they need clarity. They need to understand what prevents them from walking fully in what God has for them.

In this book, I focus on several key obstacles:

- Avoiding responsibility
- Complacency
- Letting convenience rule over commitment
- Failing to lead with love
- Cheap worship and shallow devotion
- Weakness of will
- Divided loyalty
- Neglecting to seek the Lord

These are not just theological concepts. They are spiritual realities that I have seen firsthand—in churches, in leadership teams, and in my own life. Each chapter walks through biblical examples and personal insights so that you can not only recognize these hindrances but overcome them.

Scripture As Our Source

Just like the first book, *Overcoming*

Hindrances is rooted in the unchanging truth of Scripture. Psalm 139:16 reminds us, "Your eyes saw my unformed body; all the days ordained for me were written in your book before one of them came to be." God has already ordained your days. But that doesn't mean you will live them out by default. You have to fight for what is yours in the Spirit. You must partner with God's Word and obey His leading to unlock what is already written.

That's why I revisit the stories of Ruth, Solomon, Uzziah, Jeroboam, and the lepers outside Samaria. Each of them illustrates what happens when people face a moment of choice: will they push past the hindrances—or will they settle for less than what God has in mind?

A Pastor's Perspective

As a pastor and teacher, I carry a responsibility to preach the Word not just in season, but out of season (see 2 Timothy 4:2). That means preaching truth even when it's hard to hear. Some chapters in this book may confront long-standing, well-established mindsets. They may challenge habits or beliefs you've held for a long time. But I share them in love—because I want to see you free. I want to see the Church strong. And I want to see people walk in the fullness of God's plan for their lives.

I've seen too many Christians stuck

because of fear, laziness, or misaligned priorities. They're saved—but not fruitful. They go to church—but don't carry authority. They talk about God's promises—but don't walk in them. My heart is to shake that status quo. Not with condemnation, but with conviction that leads to change.

The Road Ahead

In the chapters that follow, you will learn how to:

- Identify spiritual and practical roadblocks in your life
- Cultivate a heart of love and devotion that draws God's favor
- Break free from habits of cheap faith and surface-level obedience
- Embrace determination, loyalty, and diligence in your walk with God
- Return to the daily discipline of seeking God with all your heart.

This is not a passive book. It's a call to action. A call to rise up like the lepers in 2 Kings 7 who said, "Why sit here until we die?" It's a call to let go of excuses and embrace the inheritance that is already written for you.

Final Word

God has something incredible planned

for your life. That's not just a nice idea—it's a biblical fact. But you must take hold of it. You must fight through the distractions, the fears, and the patterns that have kept you bound. My first book reminded the reader that God's plan is real. This follow up book is your guide to removing what's blocking it.

To ensure that this book does more than inform—that it transforms—I have added three practical chapters at the end. My hope is that they will equip you not just to read about wisdom, but to practice it, share it, and pray it. If you are part of a small group, or would like to develop a prayer journal, then I have included guidelines for those practices. If you want to better practice what I am about to present, I have included an action guide for making the principles we discuss an integral part of your life.

I invite you to walk this journey with me. Let the Holy Spirit speak to you as you read. Let the Word of God cut through the confusion. And let the hindrances fall away, one by one, until you're walking fully in the calling God has placed on your life.

Let's begin.

Pastor Hiram Njoroge
Truth Bible Church
Tucson, Arizona
November 2025

CHAPTER 1

HINDRANCES TO GOD'S PLAN

Let's dive in to examine some of the hindrances that prevent us from living in the fullness of what God has promised and intended for our lives as recorded in His book. The Bible says,

> *"My frame was not hidden from you when I was made in the secret place, when I was woven together in the depths of the earth. Your eyes saw my unformed body, all the days ordained for me were written in your book before one of them came to be"* (Psalm 139:15-16).

Our days are written in His book, but we can fail to walk in or enjoy them due to hindrances that stand in the way of God's best. To begin this study, we will look at three common obstacles: failing to take responsibility, becoming complacent, and failing to let love lead.

Taking Responsibility

When you do not take responsibility, you cannot live up to God's expectations. In every generation, God calls His people to maturity. Yet many avoid responsibility by blaming others, excusing themselves, or waiting for someone else to act.

I have lived among a community of people who always seemed to blame someone else for their problems. They rarely admitted their part. They would say, "This is happening because of the government," or "It's because of my boss," or "My family didn't support me." They avoided the hard truth: "This was my fault. That is why this thing happened like this." Without responsibility, we remain spiritually immature and powerless.

In Joshua 5, Israel entered the Promised Land. For 40 years God had provided manna, food straight from heaven. But then something dramatic happened:

> *Now the children of Israel camped in Gilgal and kept the Passover on the fourteenth day of the month at twilight on the plains of Jericho. And they ate of the produce of the land on the day after the Passover, unleavened bread, and parched*

grain, on the very same day. Then the manna ceased on the day after they had eaten the produce of the land; and the children of Israel no longer had manna, but they ate the food of the land of Canaan that year (Joshua 5:10-12).

From that moment, the era of "free bread" was over. They could no longer expect God to drop food from heaven. They had to till the soil, plant crops, harvest fields, and shepherd livestock. This shift required them to accept responsibility.

Think about the imagery of the land "flowing with milk and honey." Milk doesn't fall from the sky; it requires feeding and tending goats or cows. Honey isn't poured from heaven like rain; it comes from bees, which must be cultivated or harvested. Both images imply labor, stewardship, and responsibility. God gave Israel a fruitful land, but He expected them to work it.

That same principle applies to us. Too many Christians today still want "manna Christianity." They pray that God will "drop" blessings into their lives without work, discipline, or stewardship. Some even "name and claim" other people's possessions—"I declare that house is mine!" or "I claim that car!" But you cannot take what belongs to someone else. God calls you to till your own field.

Proverbs 28:19 says it clearly: *"He*

who tills his land will have plenty of bread, but he who follows frivolity will have poverty enough." Responsibility produces provision. Laziness produces lack.

James 2 gives Abraham as an example:

But someone will say, 'You have faith; I have deeds.' Show me your faith without deeds, and I will show you my faith by my deeds. You believe that there is one God. Good! Even the demons believe that—and shudder. You foolish person, do you want evidence that faith without deeds is useless? Was not our father Abraham considered righteous for what he did when he offered his son Isaac on the altar? You see that his faith and his actions were working together, and his faith was made complete by what he did (James 2:18-22).

Abraham's faith was proven when he acted. Belief without obedience is hollow. Responsibility requires you to act on what God has spoken, even when it costs you something.

So, let us ask: Are we working the land God has given us? Are we feeding the livestock He has entrusted to us? Are we cultivating the field of our calling? If not, then we are still expecting manna to fall, when God has already called us to responsibility.

Complacency

If irresponsibility keeps us from moving forward, **complacency** keeps us stuck where we are. Complacency is the quiet enemy of growth. It whispers, "Stay where you are. Don't take risks. Don't expect more. This is as good as it gets."

But complacency is deadly to faith. It tells us that we can coast, relax, and accept the way things are. It lulls us into inactivity while God calls us to courage. One of the clearest biblical illustrations comes from 2 Kings 7, when four lepers sat outside the besieged city of Samaria:

> *Now there were four leprous men at the entrance of the gate; and they said to one another, 'Why are we sitting here until we die? If we say, "We will enter the city," the famine is in the city, and we shall die there. And if we sit here, we die also. Now therefore, come, let us surrender to the army of the Syrians. If they keep us alive, we shall live; and if they kill us, we shall only die.' And they rose at twilight to go to the camp of the Syrians; and when they had come to the outskirts of the Syrian camp, to their surprise no one was there. For the Lord had caused the army of the Syrians to hear the noise of chariots and the*

> *noise of horses—the noise of a great army; so they said to one another, 'Look, the king of Israel has hired against us the kings of the Hittites and the kings of the Egyptians to attack us!' Therefore they arose and fled at twilight, and left the camp intact—their tents, their horses, and their donkeys—and they fled for their lives"* (2 Kings 7:3-7).

These four men had less to lose than the people inside the city. They were already outcasts because of their leprosy. Yet their refusal to sit still led to God's miraculous intervention. Their footsteps were magnified into the sound of an army, causing the Syrians to flee and leaving behind an abundance of food and supplies. If they had remained complacent, they would have died. Instead, they acted—and their courage blessed an entire city.

Deuteronomy 2:24 reveals the same principle: *"Rise, take your journey, and cross over the River Arnon. Look, I have given into your hand Sihon the Amorite, king of Heshbon, and his land. Begin to possess it and engage him in battle."* Notice that God had already given the land. Yet Israel still had to rise, cross over, and engage in battle. Complacency says, "God gave it to me, so I don't need to do anything." Faith says, "God gave it to me, so I will rise and fight for it."

Jeremiah 48:11 describes complacent Moab: *"Moab has been at ease from his youth; He has settled on his dregs, and has not been emptied from vessel to vessel, nor has he gone into captivity. Therefore his taste remained in him, and his scent has not changed."*

Moab's problem was comfort. He had not been shaken or stirred, so he became stagnant and stale. And when God wanted to move him forward, Moab resisted. God will shake us, too, when we settle into complacency, because He loves us too much to leave us where we are.

Jesus reinforced this in Matthew 6:33: *"But seek first the kingdom of God and His righteousness, and all these things shall be added to you."* If we focus only on survival, security, or "things," we risk complacency. If we focus on the Kingdom, God adds what we need.

Let Love Lead

The third hindrance is **failing to let love lead.**

Many believers think they understand love, but their love is selective or conditional. They love those who look like them, think like them, or act like them. But they struggle to love across differences. This is not biblical love.

God is love (1 John 4:8). If Christ lives in us, we must embody His love. Anything less is hypocrisy. Paul reminded us, *"And now abide faith, hope, love, these three; but the greatest of these is love"* (1 Corinthians 13:13).

Jesus demonstrated this when He healed on the Sabbath, even though the Pharisees condemned Him:

> *Then He said to them, "What man is there among you who has one sheep, and if it falls into a pit on the Sabbath, will not lay hold of it and lift it out? Of how much more value then is a man than a sheep? Therefore it is lawful to do good on the Sabbath"* (Matthew 12:11-12).

The Pharisees cared more for rules and animals than for people. Jesus cared more for people than for rules. Love led His actions.

The same happened when He healed the bent-over woman in the synagogue, releasing her from years of bondage on the Sabbath (Luke 13:10-16). He reminded His critics that they would untie their ox or donkey to give it water on the Sabbath—how much more should a "daughter of Abraham" be freed from bondage? Love led Jesus to heal, serve, and sacrifice. It must lead us, too.

I recall my tradition in Kenya of visiting the elderly on my birthday. We would take blankets, food, and basic supplies to those living in dire conditions. Some were so poor they had little hope of survival. They would weep with gratitude and tell me they prayed for me daily. That experience taught me that love is not just a feeling or a theory; it is practical, sacrificial, and consistent.

Sadly, many people today are in too much of a hurry to love. They rush out of church to go home and watch TV. They claim to love God but avoid fellowship, service, or sacrifice. They may love their pets more than their neighbor's children. But true discipleship is marked by love in action. Jesus said:

> *"A new command I give you: Love one another. As I have loved you, so you must love one another. By this everyone will know that you are my disciples, if you love one another"* (John 13:34-35).

If we are not known by love, we are not known as His.

SUMMARY OF CHAPTER 1

- There are hindrances to living in the fullness of God's promises.
- We must take responsibility to steward God's blessings.
- Complacency must be confronted with faith and action.
- We must let love lead in everything we do.

Scriptures For Study And Reflection

1. **Galatians 6:4-5**
   Each one should test their own actions... for each one should carry their own load.

2. **Hebrews 10:24**
   And let us consider how we may spur one another on toward love and good deeds.

3. **Proverbs 13:4**
   A sluggard's appetite is never filled, but the desires of the diligent are fully satisfied.

4. **James 2:20, 22**
   *Faith without works is dead. . . .
   Abraham's faith was made perfect by
   his works.*

5. **John 13:34-35**
   *"Love one another. By this everyone
   will know you are my disciples."*

Discussion Questions

1. What steps can you take to assume greater responsibility for your spiritual and practical life?

2. How does complacency hinder people from stepping into God's promises?

3. What are some "battles" you need to engage in rather than waiting for God to do everything for you?

4. How does Abraham's example challenge you to combine faith with obedience?

5. In what specific ways can you let love lead in your family, church, or community?

CHAPTER 2

WHOLEHEARTED DEVOTION TO GOD

God ordained your life before you were born. His plan for you was written in His book, and your responsibility is to walk in it with an undivided heart and a willing mind. Divided loyalties, distracted thoughts, and misplaced trust can all hinder you from fully living in God's will.

David's charge to Solomon makes this clear:

> "And you, my son Solomon, acknowledge the God of your father, and serve him with wholehearted devotion and with a willing mind, for the Lord searches every heart and understands every desire and every thought. If you seek him, he will be found by you; but if you forsake him, he will reject you forever" (1 Chronicles 28:9).

Wholehearted devotion and a willing mind are not optional. They are the foundation for walking in God's plan.

A Divided Heart

David's words to Solomon show us that half-hearted devotion will never do. God does not share His throne. He is either Lord of all or not Lord at all. Jesus explained it this way:

> "What comes out of a person is what defiles them. For it is from within, out of a person's heart, that evil thoughts come—sexual immorality, theft, murder, adultery, greed, malice, deceit, lewdness, envy, slander, arrogance and folly. All these evils come from inside and defile a person" (Mark 7:20-23).

Words reveal the state of the heart. How often do people say something harsh, then quickly cover their mouths and protest, "I didn't mean that"? But once spoken, words cannot be taken back. They reveal what has been stored up in the heart.

In our culture, divided hearts are everywhere. Many want to serve both God and wealth. They trust God on Sunday but lean on their own understanding during the week. They say He is Lord, but treat Him as an "uninvited guest"—someone welcome only when convenient. But God never intrudes; He comes when invited.

David warned Solomon: if your heart is divided, your devotion will falter. If your mind is distracted, your loyalty will wander. Wholehearted devotion requires every part of us—heart, mind, strength, and soul—aligned toward God.

A Willing Mind

The second key is a willing mind. Nehemiah 4:6 records, *"So we built the wall, and the entire wall was joined together up to half its height, for the people had a mind to work."* A willing mind always unlocks extraordinary productivity. Nehemiah's wall, which had lain in ruins for years, was rebuilt in only 52 days because the people had a determined mind.

The mind is the gateway to the heart. What lingers in your thoughts eventually shapes your heart. If you dwell on fear, lust, greed, or anger, those things will sink into your heart and defile it. But if you meditate on God's Word, His truth will shape your desires and protect your heart. This is why people often say, "You can miss heaven by 12 inches"—the distance from the head to the heart. It is possible to know about God in your head but never let His Word take root in your heart.

Consider the example of sanctuary keepers. These faithful servants come early to prepare the house of God. They clean, arrange, decorate, and set the stage for worship. Few notice them, yet their willing minds produce an atmosphere of order and welcome. A willing mind does not complain about what is missing; it finds joy in serving.

Paul captures this in Colossians 3:23: *"Whatever you do, work at it with all your heart, as working for the Lord, not for human masters."* A willing mind serves God first, not human applause.

Guarding Your Heart

Wholehearted devotion means guarding the heart from corruption. Proverbs 4:23 reminds us: *"Above all else, guard your heart, for everything you do flows from it."* Your eyes and ears are gateways to the mind, and your mind is the gateway to the heart. If you allow destructive words, unholy images, or toxic attitudes to linger in your mind, they will poison your heart.

David declared: *"I have hidden your word in my heart that I might not sin against you"* (Psalm 119:11). Filling your heart with God's Word creates a filter. When lies, temptations, or distractions come, the Word acts as a barrier. Jesus reminded us that food and drink do not defile a person, but what comes from the heart does (see Mark 7:20-23). What you meditate on matters. What you watch and listen to matters. What you repeat to yourself matters. These things shape your heart and ultimately your life.

Trusting The Lord, Not Yourself

Proverbs 3:5-6 gives us the foundation for wholehearted devotion: *"Trust in the Lord with all your heart and lean not on your own understanding; in all your ways submit to him, and he will make your paths straight."* Many people today lean on paychecks, degrees, careers, or expertise. But human understanding is limited. Jobs can be lost. Paychecks can be delayed. Even expertise has limits. But God's favor never fails.

King Uzziah demonstrates this principle: *"He sought God during the days of Zechariah, who instructed him in the fear of God. As long as he sought the Lord, God gave him success"* (2 Chronicles 26:5). Uzziah's success was not rooted in his brilliance or strategies but in his devotion. He sought God, and God gave him success. The same is true for us. If we seek Him first, He directs our paths.

Practical Steps To Wholehearted Devotion

Here are some practical things you can do to enhance your ability to maintain your fervent, heartfelt devotion to the Lord:

1. **Examine your heart daily.**
   Ask, "Am I loving God with all my heart today, or am I divided?"

2. **Renew your mind through Scripture.**
   What you dwell on becomes what you desire.

3. **Filter your inputs.**
   Guard what you watch, read, and listen to—it all shapes your heart.

4. **Serve willingly.**
   Find joy in unnoticed service, like the sanctuary keepers.

5. **Seek God first.**
   Build your days around Him, not around schedules, dollars, or distractions.

SUMMARY OF CHAPTER 2

- A divided heart weakens devotion; God requires our whole heart.
- A willing mind empowers us to serve faithfully and fruitfully.
- The mind is the gateway to the heart; what we meditate on shapes our lives.
- Trust in the Lord produces true success; self-reliance produces failure.
- Wholehearted devotion requires daily choices to seek Him above all else.

Scriptures For Study And Reflection

1. **1 Chronicles 28:9**
   Serve God with wholehearted devotion and a willing mind.

2. **Nehemiah 4:6**
   The people had a mind to work.

3. **Proverbs 3:5-6**
   Trust in the Lord with all your heart and lean not on your own understanding.

4. **Psalm 119:11**
   "I have hidden your word in my heart that I might not sin against you."

5. **Mark 7:20, 23**
   "What comes out of a person defiles them . . . all these evils come from within."

Discussion Questions

1. What does wholehearted devotion look like in your current season of life?

2. In what ways can you train your mind to be more willing to serve?

3. What practical steps can you take to guard against a divided heart?

4. How can you move truth from your head into your heart more consistently?

5. Why is seeking the Lord the true foundation of success, rather than relying on expertise or resources?

CHAPTER 3

THE THREE C'S
OF JEROBOAM

The love of God is the reason why we do what we do. Why we exist is not just because of where we were born. It is because God has a purpose and a plan for our lives. But as we pursue that plan, there are hindrances that can keep us from walking in His will. Three of those hindrances appear in the life of Jeroboam, the king who led the northern tribes of Israel. I call them **the Three C's of Jeroboam: cheapness, comfort, and convenience.**

Jeroboam feared losing the loyalty of his people. Instead of trusting God, he devised his own way to keep them close. His solutions corrupted worship and set a trap for the nation.

> *Then Jeroboam built Shechem in the mountains of Ephraim, and*

dwelt there. Also he went out from there and built Penuel. And Jeroboam said in his heart, 'Now the kingdom may return to the house of David: If these people go up to offer sacrifices in the house of the Lord at Jerusalem, then the heart of this people will turn back to their lord, Rehoboam king of Judah, and they will kill me and go back to Rehoboam king of Judah.' Therefore the king asked advice, made two calves of gold, and said to the people, 'It is too much for you to go up to Jerusalem. Here are your gods, O Israel, which brought you up from the land of Egypt!' And he set up one in Bethel, and the other he put in Dan. Now this thing became a sin, for the people went to worship before the one as far as Dan (1 Kings 12:25-30).

When Jeroboam introduced these new "gods," he wasn't only setting up idols—he was establishing a pattern of cheap, comfortable, and convenient religion. That pattern still tempts us today.

1. Cheapness

Jeroboam replaced the true worship of God in Jerusalem with **cheap** substitutes in Bethel and Dan. Instead of the costly sacrifices God required, Jeroboam offered his people a bargain version of faith—one that asked less, required less, and cost less.

But true worship is never cheap. King David understood this when he sought a place to build an altar. Ornan offered him land, animals, and everything he would need for free. But David refused:

> *Then King David said to Ornan, "No, but I will surely buy it for the full price, for I will not take what is yours for the Lord, nor offer burnt offerings with that which costs me nothing." So David gave Ornan six hundred shekels of gold by weight for the place* (1 Chronicles 21:24-25).

David would not give to the Lord what cost him nothing. That principle still applies. Worship that costs us nothing is not true worship. Jesus reinforced this truth when He praised the poor widow who gave her last coin:

> *"Truly I tell you, this poor widow has put in more than all the others. All these people gave their gifts out of their wealth; but she out of her poverty put in all she had to live on"* (Luke 21:3-4).

Cheap religion gives God what is left over. True worship gives Him what is precious.

Paul modeled this attitude when he wrote: *"I will very gladly spend and be spent for your souls; though the more abundantly I love you, the less I am loved"* (2 Corinthians 12:15). Serving the Lord costs time, energy, resources, and sometimes reputation.

I remember in my early days of ministry, when money was scarce, I would walk miles to preach the gospel because I had no fare. A friend once refused to go with me, saying, "If God doesn't give me bus money, I'm not going." He stayed behind with his pillow while I walked. Along the way, dogs surrounded me. I thought they would tear me apart. But they turned on each other, fought, and left me alone. God had delivered me, and I learned again: serving Him will cost you something, but He is faithful to provide.

Cheapness is a hindrance because it reduces faith to a transaction: *"What's the minimum I can give and still look faithful?"* But worship that costs nothing is worth nothing.

2. Comfort

The second hindrance is **comfort**. Jeroboam told the people it was "too much" to go up to Jerusalem. He offered them a more comfortable option: worship close to home. But seeking God has never been about comfort. Jacob encountered God while lying on the ground with a stone for a pillow (Genesis 28:11-12). Meeting God often requires sacrifice, not luxury. Paul wrote:

> *Therefore I run thus: not with uncertainty. Thus I fight: not as one who beats the air. But I discipline my body and bring it into subjection, lest, when I have preached to others, I myself should become disqualified"* (1 Corinthians 9:26-27).

Discipleship involves discipline, not ease. Isaiah echoed this truth:

> *"If you turn away your foot from the Sabbath, from doing your pleasure on My holy day, and call the Sabbath a delight, the holy day of the Lord honorable, and shall honor Him, not doing your own ways, nor finding your own pleasure, nor speaking your own words, then you shall delight yourself in the Lord; and I will cause you to ride on the high hills of the earth, and feed you with the heritage of Jacob your father. The mouth of the Lord has spoken"* (Isaiah 58:13-14).

Too often, we let comfort dictate our service. Some won't attend church if the seats aren't padded enough or if the building isn't climate-controlled. I remember when church pews were wooden benches fixed to the floor—uncomfortable, yes, but people still came to worship.

Now many people prefer "online-only church." While livestreams can bless those who are sick or shut in, they are not a substitute for gathering with God's people. Worship is not meant to be experienced from a recliner while cooking lunch. It is meant to be shared in community, with fellowship, prayer, and the breaking of bread together.

Comfort is a poor master. If we always seek what is easy, we will never grow strong in faith.

3. Convenience

The third hindrance is **convenience**. Jeroboam built altars at Bethel and Dan so people wouldn't have to travel to Jerusalem. It was worship "close to home," designed for convenience, not obedience.

Convenience still tempts us today. Some choose a church simply because it is nearby, not because it teaches truth. Others attend where the music excites them, regardless of whether the Word is faithfully preached. Convenience is about what suits me, not what honors God.

Jesus Himself wrestled with the temptation of convenience in Gethsemane:

He went a little farther and fell on His face, and prayed, saying,

"O My Father, if it is possible, let this cup pass from Me; nevertheless, not as I will, but as You will" (Matthew 26:39).

Convenience would have led Him to walk away. Obedience led Him to the cross.

Paul charged Timothy: *"Preach the word; be prepared in season and out of season; correct, rebuke and encourage—with great patience and careful instruction"* (2 Timothy 4:2). Faithfulness is required whether it is convenient or not.

We live in a world obsessed with convenience—self-driving cars, refrigerators that order groceries, apps that anticipate our needs. These can make life easier, but they cannot shape a godly character. Spiritual growth requires effort. Salvation is not automated. You cannot "download" maturity. You must do what Abraham did, what Jesus did, what Paul did—deny yourself, take up your cross, and follow Him.

As Paul wrote: *"Therefore, my beloved, as you have always obeyed, not as in my presence only, but now much more in my absence, work out your own salvation with fear and trembling"* (Philippians 2:12).

Convenience is a snare because it lulls us into thinking discipleship should always be easy. But true obedience will cost time, energy, and sometimes even suffering.

SUMMARY OF CHAPTER 3

- We cannot be cheap when serving the Lord; worship that costs us nothing is not true worship.
- Service and fellowship may take us out of our comfort zone; discipline is required.
- Following Christ is not always convenient; we must choose obedience over ease.

Scriptures For Study And Reflection

1. 1 Kings 12:25-30
   Then Jeroboam built Shechem in the mountains of Ephraim, and dwelt there. Also he went out from there and built Penuel. And Jeroboam said in his heart, "Now the kingdom may return to the house of David: If these people go up to offer sacrifices in the house of the Lord at Jerusalem, then the heart of this people will turn back to their lord, Rehoboam king of Judah, and they will kill me and go back to Rehoboam king of Judah."

Therefore the king asked advice, made two calves of gold, and said to the people, "It is too much for you to go up to Jerusalem. Here are your gods, O Israel, which brought you up from the land of Egypt!" And he set up one in Bethel, and the other he put in Dan. Now this thing became a sin, for the people went to worship before the one as far as Dan.

2. **1 Chronicles 21:24-25**
Then King David said to Ornan, "No, but I will surely buy it for the full price, for I will not take what is yours for the Lord, nor offer burnt offerings with that which costs me nothing." So David gave Ornan six hundred shekels of gold by weight for the place.

3. **Luke 21:3-4**
"Truly I tell you," he said, "this poor widow has put in more than all the others. All these people gave their gifts out of their wealth; but she out of her poverty put in all she had to live on."

4. **Isaiah 58:13-14**
"If you turn away your foot from the Sabbath, from doing your pleasure on My holy day, and call the Sabbath a delight, the holy day of the Lord honorable, and shall honor Him, not doing your own ways, nor finding your own pleasure, nor speaking your own words, then you shall delight yourself in the

Lord; and I will cause you to ride on the high hills of the earth, and feed you with the heritage of Jacob your father. The mouth of the Lord has spoken."

5. **Philippians 2:12**
Therefore, my dear friends, as you have always obeyed—not only in my presence, but now much more in my absence—continue to work out your salvation with fear and trembling.

Discussion Questions

1. Why is worship that costs us nothing ultimately worthless in God's sight?

2. How can the pursuit of comfort hinder your walk with God?

3. In what ways does modern convenience make it harder to live a life of faith?

4. What disciplines help you resist the temptation of "cheap" or "convenient" faith?

5. How can you reorder your life to make obedience to God your priority, even when it is difficult?

CHAPTER 4

DETERMINATION, LOYALTY, AND DILIGENCE

God's plan for our lives is in His book. The psalmist declared:

> "*My frame was not hidden from you when I was made in the secret place, when I was woven together in the depths of the earth. Your eyes saw my unformed body; all the days ordained for me were written in your book before one of them came to be*" (Psalm 139:15-16).

We know that God has a plan for each of us. He wrote our manuscripts before we were born so that we would know specifically what God has for us to do. We are here for a reason. Let us look at the hindrances described in the life of Ruth and how, by trusting the Lord, she overcame them.

1. Weakness Of Will And Loyal Determination

Ruth was a biblical woman whom I love very much. She taught us that God's plans don't depend on where we came from. His plans rise above color, education, or race and surpass all human traditions and castoffs. Her story begins with deep loss:

In the days when the judges ruled, there was a famine in the land. So a man from Bethlehem in Judah, together with his wife and two sons, went to live for a while in the country of Moab. The man's name was Elimelek, his wife's name was Naomi, and the names of his two sons were Mahlon and Kilion. They were Ephrathites from Bethlehem, Judah. And they went to Moab and lived there. Now Elimelek, Naomi's husband, died, and she was left with her two sons. They married Moabite women, one named Orpah and the other Ruth. After they had lived there about ten years, both Mahlon and Kilion also died, and Naomi was left without her two sons and her husband (Ruth 1:1-5).

The family of six was reduced to three

widows—Naomi and her two daughters-in-law. With no husbands, no inheritance, and no security, Naomi urged her daughters-in-law to return to their people. Orpah kissed Naomi goodbye. But Ruth clung to her and spoke words of loyal determination that echo through the centuries:

> *"Don't urge me to leave you or to turn back from you. Where you go I will go, and where you stay I will stay. Your people will be my people and your God my God. Where you die I will die, and there I will be buried. May the Lord deal with me, be it ever so severely, if even death separates you and me"* (Ruth 1:16-17).

Ruth's determination overcame the weakness of will that might have led her back to Moab. She was willing to break tradition, embrace uncertainty, and follow Naomi into an unknown future. She chose covenant loyalty over personal comfort. Her vision lifted her above her circumstances: *"Where there is no vision, the people perish; but he that keepeth the law, happy is he"* (Proverbs 29:18).

Ruth's vision and determination made her a spiritual warrior. She would not be a castoff. She grafted herself into the people of Israel and ultimately into the lineage of Christ. Her loyalty was not passive but active—a choice that carried her into her destiny.

Determination is not just stubbornness. It is aligning your will with God's will. It is refusing to turn back when others do. It is standing firm when the easy way would be to retreat. Paul put it this way: *"Let us not become weary in doing good, for at the proper time we will reap a harvest if we do not give up"* (Galatians 6:9).

2. Laziness And Diligence

If Ruth demonstrated loyal determination in following Naomi, she also modeled diligence in her work. She did not sit around waiting for provision to come to her. She went out to glean, faithfully gathering leftover grain to feed Naomi and herself.

The overseer of the harvest told Boaz: *"She said, 'Please let me glean and gather among the sheaves behind the harvesters.' She came into the field and has remained here from morning till now, except for a short rest in the shelter"* (Ruth 2:7).

Boaz noticed her diligence and later declared: *"And now, my daughter, don't be afraid. I will do for you all you ask. All the people of my town know that you are a woman of noble character"* (Ruth 3:11).

The Bible often contrasts laziness with diligence:

- *"Lazy hands make for poverty, but diligent hands bring wealth"* (Proverbs 10:4).

- *"The plans of the diligent lead to profit as surely as haste leads to poverty"* (Proverbs 21:5).

- *"Those who work their land will have abundant food, but those who chase fantasies have no sense"* (Proverbs 12:11).

Laziness is not just physical idleness; it is spiritual neglect. Neglecting prayer, Scripture, or fellowship is a form of laziness that hinders God's plan. Diligence, on the other hand, is wholehearted application to the task God has given us.

I recall times in ministry when resources were scarce. It would have been easy to give up, to make excuses, to say, "I'll wait until conditions improve." But God blesses faithfulness in small things. When we show up, serve, study, and pray diligently, God opens doors.

Diligence is not glamorous. It is often unnoticed. But it builds character. Ruth's faithfulness in the field positioned her for favor in the house of Boaz. What we do with diligence today determines the opportunities God entrusts to us tomorrow.

3. Faithfulness

The final quality Ruth displayed was

faithfulness. Loyalty and diligence flowed from her faithfulness to God, Naomi, and the covenant she had embraced.

Faithfulness is the mark of a true steward. Paul reminded the Corinthians: *"This, then, is how you ought to regard us: as servants of Christ and as those entrusted with the mysteries God has revealed. Now it is required that those who have been given a trust must prove faithful"* (1 Corinthians 4:1-2).

Faithfulness may seem ordinary, but it is the pathway to extraordinary things. Jesus said: *"Whoever can be trusted with very little can also be trusted with much, and whoever is dishonest with very little will also be dishonest with much"* (Luke 16:10).

Paul himself is an example. Once a persecutor of the church, he later testified:

> *I thank Christ Jesus our Lord, who has given me strength, that he considered me trustworthy, appointing me to his service. Even though I was once a blasphemer and a persecutor and a violent man, I was shown mercy because I acted in ignorance and unbelief* (1 Timothy 1:12-13).

God does not demand perfection, but He requires faithfulness. Ruth was faithful in hardship, and God rewarded her. She became the great-grandmother of David and a part of Christ's lineage.

SUMMARY OF CHAPTER 4

- Determination overcomes weakness of will and fuels vision for the future.
- Diligence is the opposite of laziness; it produces honor, provision, and favor.
- Faithfulness in small things opens doors to greater responsibilities in God's kingdom.

Scriptures For Study And Reflection

1. Ruth 1:16-17
   But Ruth replied, "Don't urge me to leave you or to turn back from you. Where you go I will go, and where you stay I will stay. Your people will be my people and your God my God. Where you die I will die, and there I will be buried. May the Lord deal with me, be it ever so severely, if even death separates you and me."

2. Proverbs 29:18
   Where there is no revelation, people cast off restraint; but blessed is the one who heeds wisdom's instruction.

3. **Proverbs 10:4**

   Lazy hands make for poverty, but diligent hands bring wealth.

4. **Proverbs 21:5**

   The plans of the diligent lead to profit as surely as haste leads to poverty.

5. **1 Corinthians 4:1-2**

   This, then, is how you ought to regard us: as servants of Christ and as those entrusted with the mysteries God has revealed. Now it is required that those who have been given a trust must prove faithful.

6. **1 Timothy 1:12-13**

   I thank Christ Jesus our Lord, who has given me strength, that he considered me trustworthy, appointing me to his service. Even though I was once a blasphemer and a persecutor and a violent man, I was shown mercy because I acted in ignorance and unbelief.

7. **Luke 16:10**

   "Whoever can be trusted with very little can also be trusted with much, and whoever is dishonest with very little will also be dishonest with much."

Discussion Questions

1. Ruth chose loyalty when Orpah turned back. What does this teach us about determination in difficult times?

2. In what areas of your life are you

tempted to be spiritually or practically lazy? How can diligence change that?

3. How have you experienced God's favor after a season of consistent faithfulness?

4. Why does God place such high value on faithfulness in small things?

5. Which of these three traits—determination, diligence, or faithfulness—is God asking you to grow in today?

6. What practical steps can you take this week to align your will, your work, and your loyalty with God's plan?

CHAPTER 5

FIGHTING SETBACKS

Joseph had a dream and told it to his brothers. After that, they hated him even more. Through this we learn that even if you think you did not start off well, you can still fulfill the purpose God has written for you. Setbacks are not the end of God's plan—they are often the proving ground for it.

1. Not Starting Off Well

We are going to live every day that the Lord wrote in His book. The next hindrance we will look at is **not starting off well.** Joseph did not begin his journey with favor in his family. In fact, his story shows us that even those closest to us may misunderstand or oppose the vision God has placed within us.

Now Jacob dwelt in the land where his father was a stranger, in the land of Canaan. This is the history of Jacob. Joseph, being seventeen years old, was feeding the flock with his brothers. And the lad was with the sons of Bilhah and the sons of Zilpah, his father's wives; and Joseph brought a bad report of them to his father. Now Israel loved Joseph more than all his children, because he was the son of his old age; also he made him a tunic of many colors. But when his brothers saw that their father loved him more than all his brothers, they hated him and could not speak peaceably to him (Genesis 37:1-4).

Jealousy poisoned Joseph's relationships. His brothers mocked him: *"Then they said to one another, 'Look, this dreamer is coming!'"* (Genesis 37:19). They hated his dreams because his dreams revealed God's destiny for his life.

"Come therefore, let us now kill him and cast him into some pit; and we shall say, 'Some wild beast has devoured him.' We shall see what will become of his dreams" (Genesis 37:20).

Joseph did not start off well. Neither did Moses.

And a man of the house of Levi went and took as wife a daughter of

Levi. So the woman conceived and bore a son. And when she saw that he was a beautiful child, she hid him three months. But when she could no longer hide him, she took an ark of bulrushes for him, daubed it with asphalt and pitch, put the child in it, and laid it in the reeds by the river's bank (Exodus 2:1-3).

Moses was hunted from day one. His life began in crisis. But God's hand was upon him, just as it was upon Joseph.

This is a crucial lesson: even if you did not start well, God's dreams for you can carry you. Sometimes your vision seems too big for you to hold, but when it comes from God, it holds you. I think of the many who feel their beginnings disqualify them: a broken family, a poor education, a failure in youth. Yet in God's book, your destiny is not canceled by your beginning. God delights in rewriting stories and using broken vessels.

2. Surprises

Our journey can be full of **surprises** that feel like setbacks. When surprises come, we think we are the only ones who have ever faced them. But Joseph's life teaches us that God can use even shocking betrayals to advance His plan.

So it came to pass, when Joseph had come to his brothers, that they stripped Joseph of his tunic, the tunic of many colors that was on him. Then they took him and cast him into a pit. And the pit was empty; there was no water in it. And they sat down to eat a meal. Then they lifted their eyes and looked, and there was a company of Ishmaelites, coming from Gilead with their camels, bearing spices, balm, and myrrh, on their way to carry them down to Egypt. So Judah said to his brothers, "What profit is there if we kill our brother and conceal his blood? Come and let us sell him to the Ishmaelites, and let not our hand be upon him, for he is our brother and our flesh." And his brothers listened (Genesis 37:23-27).

That was Joseph's "reward" for faithfully going to his brothers with food: betrayal, rejection, and being sold into slavery. Life can surprise us the same way—sudden sickness, unexpected betrayal, job loss, or financial hardship. Yet even in Egypt, God reversed Joseph's situation:

"The Lord was with Joseph, and he was a successful man; and he was in the house of his master the Egyptian" (Genesis 39:2).

The Lord was with Joseph in the pit, in

Potiphar's house, and later in prison. God's presence turned setbacks into stepping stones.

Sometimes surprises look like detours, but they are often God's re-directions. Surprises remind us that we are not in control, but they also remind us that God is never surprised.

3. Rejection

Perhaps the most painful setback of all is **rejection**. Rejection wounds deeply and tempts us to give up. Joseph experienced this at the hands of Potiphar's wife, who falsely accused him of a crime he did not commit:

> So it was, when his master heard the words which his wife spoke to him, saying, "Your servant did to me after this manner," that his anger was aroused. Then Joseph's master took him and put him into the prison, a place where the king's prisoners were confined (Genesis 39:19-20).

Joseph spent years in prison, forgotten by those he had helped. Yet God did not abandon him:

> But the Lord was with Joseph and showed him mercy, and He gave him favor in the sight of the keeper of the prison. And the keeper of the

> *prison committed to Joseph's hand all the prisoners who were in the prison; whatever they did there, it was his doing. The keeper of the prison did not look into anything that was under Joseph's authority, because the Lord was with him; and whatever he did, the Lord made it prosper"*(Genesis 39:21-23).

Job also knew rejection, as did Jeremiah, as did Jesus Himself. Rejection never feels good, but it never removes God's presence. God is too good to be unkind and too wise to be mistaken. Even in rejection, He remains faithful.

When you feel abandoned or mis-understood, remember Joseph: rejected by brothers, betrayed by Potiphar's wife, forgotten in prison—yet never forsaken by God.

SUMMARY OF CHAPTER 5

- Even if you did not start off well, God's plan can still be fulfilled.
- Surprises may shake you, but they cannot remove God's presence.
- Rejection is painful, but God never abandons you.

Scriptures For Study And Reflection

1. Genesis 37:1-5

   Now Jacob dwelt in the land where his father was a stranger, in the land of Canaan. This is the history of Jacob. Joseph, being seventeen years old, was feeding the flock with his brothers. And the lad was with the sons of Bilhah and the sons of Zilpah, his father's wives; and Joseph brought a bad report of them to his father. Now Israel loved Joseph more than all his children, because he was the son of his old age; also he made him a tunic of many colors. But when his brothers saw that . . .

2. **Genesis 37:19-20**

   Then they said to one another, "Look, this dreamer is coming! Come therefore, let us now kill him and cast him into some pit; and we shall say, 'Some wild beast has devoured him.' We shall see what will become of his dreams."

3. **Exodus 2:1-3**

   And a man of the house of Levi went and took as wife a daughter of Levi. So the woman conceived and bore a son. And when she saw that he was a beautiful child, she hid him three months. But when she could no longer hide him, she took an ark of bulrushes for him, daubed it with asphalt and pitch, put the child in it, and laid it in the reeds by the river's bank.

4. **Genesis 39:2**

   The Lord was with Joseph, and he was a successful man; and he was in the house of his master the Egyptian.

5. **Genesis 39:21-23**

   But the Lord was with Joseph and showed him mercy, and He gave him favor in the sight of the keeper of the prison. And the keeper of the prison committed to Joseph's hand all the prisoners who were in the prison; whatever they did there, it was his doing. The keeper of the prison did not look into anything that was under Joseph's authority, because the Lord was with him; and whatever he did, the Lord made it prosper.

Discussion Questions

1. How does Joseph's story encourage you when you feel your beginnings are against you?

2. What "surprises" in your life have turned into God's re-directions?

3. How can you remind yourself of God's presence when facing rejection?

4. Why is it important to see setbacks as part of God's shaping process?

5. Which setback—poor beginnings, surprises, or rejection—do you most relate to right now?

6. How can Joseph's example help you endure until God's plan unfolds fully in your life?

CHAPTER 6

BATTLING LIMITATIONS

While studying circumstances which hinder us from living the purposes of God, we can look at the life of Moses. When Moses went to Midian, Jethro welcomed him to his home and gave him one of his daughters to be his wife. Scripture says that Moses was content to live in the house of Jethro.

Contentment is not always a blessing. Sometimes it can become a hindrance. When we settle in too comfortably, we risk losing sight of God's call to move forward. If we become insecure, unwilling, or unable to take the next step, apparent limitations can make the future look bleak. But with God's help, limitations do not have to define us.

1. Family Criticisms

The first obstacles we often face come from family. Before the world resists us, our closest relatives sometimes doubt us, criticize us, or attempt to define our future for us. God reminded Samuel of His perspective:

> *"Do not consider his appearance or his height, for I have rejected him. The Lord does not look at the things people look at. People look at the outward appearance, but the Lord looks at the heart"* (1 Samuel 16:7).

Joseph is a clear example of family criticism and rejection:

> *But when his brothers saw that their father loved him more than all his brothers, they hated him and could not speak peaceably to him. Now Joseph had a dream, and he told it to his brothers, and they hated him even more. So he said to them, "Please hear this dream which I have dreamed: There we were, binding sheaves in the field. Then behold, my sheaf arose and also stood upright; and indeed your sheaves stood all around and bowed down to my sheaf." And his brothers said to him, 'Shall you indeed reign over us? Or shall you indeed have dominion over us?' So they hated him even more for his dreams and for his words* (Genesis 37:4-8).

His own family plotted against him, yet God lifted Joseph to become prime minister of Egypt, saving the very family that had despised him. Family limitations could not prevent God's purpose.

David also faced family dismissal. When Samuel came to anoint Israel's first king, Jesse paraded all his other sons before the prophet, never considering David. Yet Samuel insisted:

> *So he asked Jesse, "Are these all the sons you have?" "There is still the youngest" Jesse answered. "He is tending the sheep." Samuel said, "Send for him; we will not sit down until he arrives." So he sent for him and had him brought in. He was glowing with health and had a fine appearance and handsome features. Then the Lord said, "Rise and anoint him; this is the one"* (1 Samuel 16:11-12).

Family saw a shepherd boy; God saw a king.

Jabez is another striking case. His very name marked him with limitation:

> *Now Jabez was more honorable than his brothers, and his mother called his name Jabez, saying, "Because I bore him in pain." And Jabez called on the God of Israel saying, "Oh, that You would bless*

me indeed, and enlarge my territo-
ry, that Your hand would be with
me, and that You would keep me
from evil, that I may not cause
pain!" So God granted him what he
requested (1 Chronicles 4:9-10).

Though born with a name meaning "pain," Jabez overcame family limitations through prayer.

Even Benjamin's destiny was contested at birth. Rachel named him Ben-Oni, "son of my sorrow," but Jacob renamed him Benjamin, "son of my right hand" (Genesis 35:18). A father's blessing redirected his future away from grief toward strength. Family criticisms may be real, but God's calling always outweighs them.

2. Occupational Limitations

Occupational limitations can hinder us just as much as family. Not everyone feels qualified, trained, or prepared for the work before them. Inadequacy at work or in ministry often tempts us to retreat. From the beginning, work has been God's design. Adam was placed in Eden *"to work it and take care of it"* (Genesis 2:15). Yet every occupation comes with challenges—lack of opportunity, lack of training, lack of resources.

David faced occupational limitations when confronting Goliath. To the trained soldiers, he was just a shepherd boy, unfit for the battlefield. His brothers mocked him; Saul doubted him. Yet David refused to let their judgment define him.

> *David said to Saul, "Your servant has been keeping his father's sheep. When a lion or a bear came and carried off a sheep from the flock, I went after it, struck it and rescued the sheep from its mouth. When it turned on me, I seized it by its hair, struck it and killed it. Your servant has killed both the lion and the bear; this uncircumcised Philistine will be like one of them, because he has defied the armies of the living God"* (1 Samuel 17:34-36).

Others saw a boy with a sling. David saw a servant of God empowered to act on behalf of his people.

Occupational limitations today may look like a lack of credentials, experience, or confidence. But with the Spirit of God, ordinary people do extraordinary things. Paul reminds us: *"I can do all things through Christ who strengthens me"* (Philippians 4:13).

3. Battlefield Limitations

Sometimes the greatest limitations appear when we are thrust onto the battlefield—spiritual or otherwise. The enemy mocks our weakness and magnifies our shortcomings.

And when the Philistine looked about and saw David, he disdained him; for he was only a youth, ruddy and good-looking. So the Philistine said to David, "Am I a dog, that you come to me with sticks?" And the Philistine cursed David by his gods. And the Philistine said to David, 'Come to me, and I will give your flesh to the birds of the air and the beasts of the field" (1 Samuel 17:42-44).

David may have seemed unqualified—too young, too small, too poorly armed—yet he declared victory in God's name. His sling was enough because his faith was strong. Paul later explained: *"The weapons of our warfare are not carnal but mighty in God for pulling down strongholds"* (2 Corinthians 10:4).

Hannah knew how to fight on the battlefield of prayer. Though misunderstood in the temple, her silent cries reached heaven (1 Samuel 1:12-13). God heard her unspoken words and answered.

Ezekiel too was strengthened for spiritual battle:

"But the Lord said to me: 'Behold, I have made your face strong against their faces, and your forehead strong against their foreheads. Like adamant stone, harder than flint, I

*have made your forehead; do not
be afraid of them, nor be dismayed
at their looks, though they are a rebellious house'"* (Ezekiel 3:8-9).

Limitations on the battlefield high-
light our dependence on God. Our strength
is not in our weapons, but in His Word and
Spirit.

SUMMARY OF CHAPTER 6

- Family criticisms may limit you, but God looks at the heart and can rewrite your destiny.
- Occupational limitations can be overcome when you trust God's power instead of human qualifications.
- Battlefield limitations remind us that our weapons are spiritual and our victory comes from God.

Scriptures For Study And Reflection

1. **1 Samuel 16:7**
   But the Lord said to Samuel, "Do not consider his appearance or his height, for I have rejected him. The Lord does not look at the things people look at. People look at the outward appearance, but the Lord looks at the heart."

2. **Genesis 37:4-8**
   But when his brothers saw that their father loved him more than all his brothers, they hated him and could not speak

peaceably to him. Now Joseph had a dream, and he told it to his brothers, and they hated him even more. So he said to them, "Please hear this dream which I have dreamed: There we were, binding sheaves in the field. Then behold, my sheaf arose and also stood upright; and indeed your sheaves stood all around and bowed down to my sheaf." And his brothers said to him, "Shall you indeed reign over us? Or shall you indeed have dominion over us?" So they hated him even more for his dreams and for his words.

3. **1 Chronicles 4:9-10**

   Now Jabez was more honorable than his brothers, and his mother called his name Jabez, saying, "Because I bore him in pain." And Jabez called on the God of Israel saying, "Oh, that You would bless me indeed, and enlarge my territory, that Your hand would be with me, and that You would keep me from evil, that I may not cause pain!" So God granted him what he requested.

4. **Genesis 35:18**

   And so it was, as her soul was departing (for she died), that she called his name Ben-Oni; but his father called him Benjamin.

5. **1 Samuel 17:34-36**

   But David said to Saul, "Your servant

used to keep his father's sheep, and when a lion or a bear came and took a lamb out of the flock, I went out after it and struck it, and delivered the lamb from its mouth; and when it arose against me, I caught it by its beard, and struck and killed it. Your servant has killed both lion and bear; and this uncircumcised Philistine will be like one of them, seeing he has defied the armies of the living God."

6. 2 Corinthians 10:4

For the weapons of our warfare are not carnal but mighty in God for pulling down strongholds.

7. Ezekiel 3:8-9

Behold, I have made your face strong against their faces, and your forehead strong against their foreheads. Like adamant stone, harder than flint, I have made your forehead; do not be afraid of them, nor be dismayed at their looks, though they are a rebellious house.

Discussion Questions

1. How have family criticisms or limitations shaped your view of yourself, and how can God's perspective redefine you?

2. What occupational limitations do you face, and how can you apply David's example of courage to them?

3. What does it mean for you to fight with "spiritual weapons" rather than human strength?

4. How does the story of Jabez encourage you to pray boldly against family-imposed labels?

5. When have you experienced a "battlefield limitation," and how did faith help you overcome it?

6. Which of these three limitations — family, occupational, or battlefield — is most pressing for you today, and how can you surrender it to God?

CHAPTER 7

TYPES OF WISDOM

God is a good and loving Father. We are His children, and we are loved. One of the greatest requirements for living successfully in His will is wisdom—the right application of knowledge. It is not merely how much we know but how we apply what we know. The Bible teaches that wisdom comes in more than one form:

> *This wisdom does not descend from above, but is earthly, sensual, demonic. For where envy and self-seeking exist, confusion and every evil thing are there. But the wisdom that is from above is first pure, then peaceable, gentle, willing to yield, full of mercy and good fruits, without partiality and without hypocrisy* (James 3:15-17).

Let's examine four categories of wisdom, then honestly gauge ourselves to see where we operate.

1. Earthly Or Natural Wisdom

The first category is **earthly wisdom**—what we might call common sense or natural instinct. It is the ability built into our very design as human beings.

A newborn child instinctively knows how to feed. No one teaches a baby to cry when hungry or to latch on to its mother's breast. That is earthly wisdom. Similarly, a hungry man does not debate hunger; he finds food. Our bodies remind us when we need rest, water, or warmth. These are natural impulses built into our humanity.

This kind of wisdom has value, but it is limited to earthly outcomes. Natural wisdom can help you survive, but it cannot help you discern the purposes of God. Paul described those who live only by the natural: *"The person without the Spirit does not accept the things that come from the Spirit of God but considers them foolishness"* (1 Corinthians 2:14).

We need wisdom beyond instinct. Natural wisdom is good for eating when hungry or avoiding fire when it burns, but it cannot guide you into eternal life.

2. Intellectual Wisdom

The second category is **intellectual wisdom**—the exercise of the mind. This comes from study, reflection, and mentorship. It is found in books, education, and the pursuit of learning. Daniel grew in this kind of wisdom:

> *In the first year of his reign I, Daniel, understood by the books the number of the years specified by the word of the Lord through Jeremiah the prophet, that He would accomplish seventy years in the desolations of Jerusalem"* (Daniel 9:2).

Daniel sought knowledge through study and was blessed with understanding. Intellectual wisdom is cultivated whenever you read, research, or sit under teaching.

Yet intellectual wisdom has its limits. It can puff up without love (1 Corinthians 8:1). It can lead to arrogance, as when young students think they know more than their parents because they have learned a new formula. Moses himself *"was learned in all the wisdom of the Egyptians, and was mighty in words and deeds"* (Acts 7:22). Yet his Egyptian training led him to kill a man and spend 40 years in the wilderness.

Intellectual wisdom without God is dangerous. Paul warned Timothy: *"But you must continue in the things which you have learned and been assured of, knowing from whom you have learned them"* (2 Timothy 3:14). Mentorship matters. Head knowledge without spiritual guidance leads to pride and poor decisions.

Intellectual wisdom can be a gift when used with humility. But it becomes a hindrance when it convinces us that we are wiser than God.

3. Devilish Wisdom

The third category is **devilish wisdom**. This may sound strange, but Scripture warns of wisdom that is not from God. Pharaoh sought it when he called for magicians to interpret his dream:

> *Now it came to pass in the morning that his spirit was troubled, and he sent and called for all the magicians of Egypt and all its wise men. And Pharaoh told them his dreams, but there was no one who could interpret them for Pharaoh* (Genesis 41:8).

Occult practices, fortune telling, and sorcery fall into this category. They rely on spiritual powers but not the Spirit of God. They can reveal things about your past or even your name, but they cannot reveal God's truth. They seduce people away from the narrow path with counterfeits.

Paul himself was once led by this kind of zeal without knowledge. As Saul, he thought he was wise, but his wisdom was destructive, persecuting the church of Christ. Devilish wisdom can appear powerful, but it leads to confusion and bondage.

The good news is that in Christ we have authority to confront devilish wisdom. Paul wrote: *"For though we live in the world, we do not wage war as the world does. The weapons we fight with are not the weapons of the world. On the contrary, they have divine power to demolish strongholds"* (2 Corinthians 10:3-4).

We must resist devilish wisdom, for it masquerades as light but leads to darkness.

4. Wisdom From Above

The fourth and highest category is **wisdom from above**. This is the wisdom that comes directly from God, through His Word and Spirit. Proverbs describes wisdom's voice:

"By me kings reign, and rulers decree justice; by me princes rule, and nobles, all who judge rightly" (Proverbs 8:15-16).

This wisdom builds lives and households:

Through wisdom a house is built, and by understanding it is established; by knowledge the rooms are filled with all precious and pleasant riches. A wise man is strong, yes, a man of knowledge increases strengt" (Proverbs 24:3-5).

Wisdom from above is practical. It is not just about decisions in church but also about managing families, finances, relationships, and communities. It is strength for daily living. Ecclesiastes illustrates its power:

> *There was a small city with few men in it; and a great king came against it, besieged it, and built large siegeworks against it. But there was found in it a poor wise man, and he by his wisdom delivered the city. Yet no one remembered that poor man* (Ecclesiastes 9:14-15).

It's not wealth, status, or power that saves, but wisdom. Ultimately, the wisdom from above is revealed in Christ Himself:

> *But to those whom God has called, both Jews and Greeks, Christ the power of God and the wisdom of God* (1 Corinthians 1:24).

Christ is the wisdom of God. When we invite Him into our lives, His Spirit dwells within us, guiding us into truth. This wisdom surpasses natural, intellectual, and even spiritual counterfeits. It is pure, peaceable, merciful, and without hypocrisy (James 3:17). Jude closes his letter with this doxology:

> *To God our Savior, who alone is wise, be glory and majesty, dominion and power, both now and forever. Amen* (Jude 1:25).

The question is simple: Which wisdom do you operate in? Natural instinct, intellectual learning, counterfeit spiritualism, or the wisdom from above that only comes through Christ?

SUMMARY OF CHAPTER 7

- Wisdom is necessary for successfully living in God's will and purpose.
- There are four types of wisdom: Natural, Intellectual, Devilish, and From Above.
- Only wisdom from above leads to life, strength, and eternal reward.
- Christ Himself is the wisdom of God, and He offers that wisdom to all who receive Him.

Scriptures For Study And Reflection

1. **James 3:15-17**
   This wisdom does not descend from above, but is earthly, sensual, demonic. For where envy and self-seeking exist, confusion and every evil thing are there. But the wisdom that is from above is first pure, then peaceable, gentle, willing to yield, full of mercy and good fruits, without partiality and without hypocrisy.

2. **Daniel 9:2**
   In the first year of his reign I, Daniel,

understood by the books the number of the years specified by the word of the Lord through Jeremiah the prophet, that He would accomplish seventy years in the desolations of Jerusalem.

3. Acts 7:22

   Moses was educated in all the wisdom of the Egyptians and was powerful in speech and action.

4. Genesis 41:8

   Now it came to pass in the morning that his spirit was troubled, and he sent and called for all the magicians of Egypt and all its wise men. And Pharaoh told them his dreams, but there was no one who could interpret them for Pharaoh.

5. Proverbs 24:3-5

   Through wisdom a house is built, and by understanding it is established; by knowledge the rooms are filled with all precious and pleasant riches. A wise man is strong, yes, a man of knowledge increases strength.

6. Ecclesiastes 9:14-15

   There was a small city with few men in it; and a great king came against it, besieged it, and built large siegeworks against it. But there was found in it a poor wise man, and he by his wisdom delivered the city. Yet no one remembered that poor man.

7. **1 Corinthians 1:24**
   But to those whom God has called, both Jews and Greeks, Christ the power of God and the wisdom of God.

8. **Jude 1:25**
   To God our Savior, who alone is wise, be glory and majesty, dominion and power, both now and forever. Amen.

Discussion Questions

1. How do you see the difference between natural instinct and true wisdom from above?

2. What are the strengths and dangers of intellectual wisdom in today's world?

3. Why is it important to recognize and resist devilish wisdom?

4. How can wisdom from above strengthen your family, work, and spiritual life?

5. In what ways does Christ demonstrate the wisdom of God in your own life?

6. Which category of wisdom do you most often rely on, and how can you grow in wisdom from above?

CHAPTER 8

WISE LEADERS

Wisdom is a pure gift from God, available to all His children. Like any gift, it cannot be earned; it must be received. A gift must also be accepted—if you never take hold of it, you do not benefit from it. Wisdom is essential to life because it shapes how we apply knowledge in every decision. Scripture emphasizes wisdom's value:

> *Wisdom is good with an inheritance, and profitable to those who see the sun* (Ecclesiastes 7:11).

> *By wisdom a house is built, and through understanding it is established; through knowledge its rooms are filled with rare and beautiful treasures* (Proverbs 24:3-4).

> *Wisdom is the principal thing; therefore get wisdom. And in all your getting, get understanding* (Proverbs 4:7, NKJV).

Wisdom is not optional; it is the foundation of successful living and leadership. Let us consider four biblical leaders who demonstrate wisdom: Joseph, Solomon, Daniel, and Paul.

1. Joseph: Wisdom That Elevates

Joseph's life illustrates how divine wisdom **elevates** us beyond circumstances. Hated by his brothers, sold into slavery, and falsely accused, Joseph spent years in hardship. Yet in every setting—Potiphar's house, prison, and Pharaoh's court—the wisdom of God was evident. When Pharaoh had troubling dreams, Joseph was summoned:

> *And Pharaoh said to Joseph, "I have had a dream, and there is no one who can interpret it. But I have heard it said of you that you can understand a dream, to interpret it." So Joseph answered Pharaoh, saying, "It is not in me; God will give Pharaoh an answer of peace"* (Genesis 41:15-16).

Joseph's wisdom was not self-generated. He gave glory to God as the source of interpretation and counsel. Pharaoh recognized this:

> *So Pharaoh asked them, "Can we find anyone like this man, one in whom is the Spirit of God?" Then Pharaoh said to Joseph, "Since God*

has made all this known to you, there is no one so discerning and wise as you. You shall be in charge of my palace, and all my people are to submit to your orders. Only with respect to the throne will I be greater than you" (Genesis 41:38-40).

Wisdom lifted Joseph from the prison to the palace. His leadership saved nations from famine. This reminds us that godly wisdom is not for personal gain but for the benefit of others. Proverbs affirms: *"By me kings reign and rulers decree justice; by me princes rule, and nobles—all who govern justly"* (Proverbs 8:15-16).

Joseph rose not by connections, wealth, or power but by divine wisdom. That same wisdom is available to us.

2. Solomon: Wisdom Above Riches

Whenever wisdom is mentioned, Solomon comes to mind. He understood that wisdom is the true measure of success and not wealth or **riches**. When God offered him anything, Solomon asked only for wisdom:

"Give me wisdom and knowledge, that I may lead this people, for who is able to govern this great people of yours?" (2 Chronicles 1:10).

God was pleased:

God said to Solomon, "Since this is

your heart's desire and you have not asked for wealth, possessions or honor, nor for the death of your enemies, and since you have not asked for a long life but for wisdom and knowledge to govern my people. . . . Therefore wisdom and knowledge will be given you. And I will also give you wealth, possessions and honor, such as no king who was before you ever had and none after you will have" (2 Chronicles 1:11-12).

Solomon's story reminds us that when wisdom is sought first, God often adds other blessings. His wisdom surpassed all around him:

God gave Solomon wisdom and very great insight, and a breadth of understanding as measureless as the sand on the seashore. Solomon's wisdom was greater than the wisdom of all the people of the East, and greater than all the wisdom of Egypt (1 Kings 4:29-30).

Wisdom gave Solomon the ability to judge justly, as seen in the famous case of the two women disputing a child (1 Kings 3:16-28). It also allowed him to build the temple, write proverbs, and instruct nations.

Wisdom does not prevent mistakes—Solomon later stumbled when he allowed foreign wives to turn his heart—but his example shows how highly God values wisdom when it is sought above all else.

3. Daniel: Wisdom That Distinguishes

Daniel's life in Babylon highlights how godly **wisdom distinguishes** believers even in hostile environments. Though he was trained in Babylonian culture and knowledge, Daniel drew his true wisdom from God.

> *As for these four young men, God gave them knowledge and skill in all literature and wisdom; and Daniel had understanding in all visions and dreams. Now at the end of the days, when the king had said that they should be brought in, the chief of the eunuchs brought them in before Nebuchadnezzar. Then the king interviewed them, and among them all none was found like Daniel, Hananiah, Mishael, and Azariah; therefore they served before the king. And in all matters of wisdom and understanding about which the king examined them, he found them ten times better than all the magicians and astrologers who were in all his realm* (Daniel 1:17-20).

Daniel's wisdom set him apart from his peers. He was able to serve under four kings because he consistently relied on God for understanding.

When Nebuchadnezzar had dreamed dreams that baffled his wise men, Daniel sought God:

> *Then the secret was revealed to Daniel in a night vision. So Daniel blessed the God of heaven"* (Daniel 2:19).

Daniel acknowledged God as the source of wisdom:

> *"He gives wisdom to the wise and knowledge to the discerning. He reveals deep and hidden things; he knows what lies in darkness, and light dwells with him"* (Daniel 2:21-22).

Daniel's life shows that divine wisdom can flourish even in exile, in workplaces that do not honor God, and under rulers who do not believe. Wisdom from above shines brightest in dark places.

4. Paul: Wisdom That Explains Christ

Paul's life is another testament to **divine wisdom.** Unlike Peter, who walked with Jesus, Paul came later—once a persecutor of the church, then a preacher of Christ. His writings carry profound wisdom that even astonished the original apostles. Peter himself testified,

> *Bear in mind that our Lord's patience means salvation, just as our dear brother Paul also wrote you with the wisdom that God gave him. He writes the same way in all his letters, speaking in them of these matters. His letters contain some things that are hard to understand, which ignorant and unstable people distort, as they do the other Scriptures, to their own destruction* (2 Peter 3:15-16).

Peter, who had walked with Jesus, admitted that Paul's writings were difficult yet full of God-given wisdom.

Paul described his own ministry this way:

> *According to the grace of God which was given to me, as a wise master builder I laid a foundation, and another builds on it. But each one must be careful how he builds on it. For no one can lay any foundation other than the one already laid, which is Jesus Christ* (1 Corinthians 3:10-11).

Though late to the apostolic calling, Paul became one of the most influential voices in the church. His wisdom clarified the gospel, explained Christ's death and resurrection, and gave structure to the early church.

This teaches us that wisdom is not about how early you start but how faithful you are once God calls you.

SUMMARY OF CHAPTER 8

- Joseph received wisdom from God and rose from prisoner to prime minister.
- Solomon sought wisdom above all else, and God gave him wisdom along with wealth and honor.
- Daniel's wisdom set him apart, enabling him to serve faithfully through multiple regimes.
- Paul's writings carried divine wisdom that even the apostles recognized as extraordinary.
- Wisdom from above equips leaders to guide, protect, and strengthen God's people.

Scriptures For Study And Reflection

1. **Ecclesiastes 7:11**
   Wisdom is good with an inheritance, and profitable to those who see the sun.

2. **Proverbs 24:3-4**
   By wisdom a house is built, and through understanding it is established; through

knowledge its rooms are filled with rare and beautiful treasures.

3. **Proverbs 4:7**
    Wisdom is the principal thing; therefore get wisdom. And in all your getting, get understanding.

4. **Genesis 41:15-16**
    And Pharaoh said to Joseph, "I have had a dream, and there is no one who can interpret it. But I have heard it said of you that you can understand a dream, to interpret it." So Joseph answered Pharaoh, saying, "It is not in me; God will give Pharaoh an answer of peace."

5. **1 Kings 4:29-30**
    God gave Solomon wisdom and very great insight, and a breadth of understanding as measureless as the sand on the seashore. Solomon's wisdom was greater than the wisdom of all the people of the East, and greater than all the wisdom of Egypt.

6. **Daniel 1:17-20**
    As for these four young men, God gave them knowledge and skill in all literature and wisdom; and Daniel had understanding in all visions and dreams. ... In all matters of wisdom and understanding about which the king examined them, he found them ten times better than all the magicians and astrologers who were in all his realm.

7. **2 Peter 3:15-16**

Our dear brother Paul also wrote you with the wisdom that God gave him. ... His letters contain some things that are hard to understand, which ignorant and unstable people distort, as they do the other Scriptures, to their own destruction.

8. **1 Corinthians 3:10-11**

According to the grace of God which was given to me, as a wise master builder I laid a foundation, and another builds on it. But each one must be careful how he builds on it. For no one can lay any foundation other than the one already laid, which is Jesus Christ.

Discussion Questions

1. Joseph rose from prisoner to ruler because of wisdom. How can God's wisdom elevate you in your current situation?

2. Solomon asked for wisdom above riches or power. What does this teach us about what to value most in prayer?

3. How can Daniel's example help you stand out with integrity in environments that do not honor God?

4. Why is Paul's wisdom—even greater than Peter expected—important for the church today?

5. What does it mean for you person-
    ally to "get wisdom" as Proverbs 4:7
    commands?

6. Which of these biblical examples—
    Joseph, Solomon, Daniel, Paul—most
    challenges you to seek divine wisdom?

CHAPTER 9

WAYS TO GAIN WISDOM

Jesus invites us to pursue wisdom with bold persistence:

"Ask, and it will be given to you; seek, and you will find; knock, and it will be opened to you. For everyone who asks receives, and he who seeks finds, and to him who knocks it will be opened" (Matthew 7:7-8).

James echoes this promise:

If any of you lacks wisdom, let him ask of God, who gives to all liberally and without reproach, and it will be given to him (James 1:5).

Wisdom is not automatic. It comes when we ask, seek, and knock. God knows our problems, but He waits for us to invite Him into them. Until we seek His wisdom, we may remain stuck. Let us look at four ways we can gain divine wisdom.

1. Seek Wisdom Through Prayer

Prayer is the first gateway to wisdom. Too often, people see prayer as a ritual—a list of requests, a set of memorized words, or an emergency hotline to heaven. Some travel long distances for someone else to lay hands on them, thinking wisdom comes through human touch. But true prayer is not magic. It is worship, relationship, and communion with God.

James wrote, *"If any of you lacks wisdom, let him ask of God, who gives to all liberally and without reproach, and it will be given to him"* (James 1:5, NKJV). Wisdom must be requested. God does not force it upon us. He delights to give it, but He gives it to those who ask. Paul's prayer for the Colossians illustrates this:

> *For this reason we also, since the day we heard it, do not cease to pray for you, and to ask that you may be filled with the knowledge of His will in all wisdom and spiritual understanding* (Colossians 1:9).

True prayer asks not just for blessings but for wisdom to know God's will. Jeremiah 33:3 reinforces this promise: *"Call to Me, and I will answer you, and show you great and mighty things, which you do not know."*

When we pray, let us ask not simply for provision or healing, but for wisdom to understand God's purposes.

2. Seek Wisdom Through Learning

The second pathway to wisdom is **learning**. Prayer and learning go hand in hand. A person who stops learning has chosen stagnation. Proverbs declares: *"A wise man will hear and increase learning, and a man of understanding will attain wise counsel"* (Proverbs 1:5).

Learning requires humility—the humility to admit that we do not know everything, and the discipline to keep growing. Paul, even as an apostle, requested his books and parchments:

> *Bring the cloak that I left with Carpus at Troas when you come— and the books, especially the parchments* (2 Timothy 4:13).

Paul never stopped reading, reflecting, and learning. Too many today replace serious study with scrolling social media. They skim headlines or memes but rarely sit with Scripture. That kind of "learning" cannot impart wisdom.

Daniel grew wise through study:

> *In the first year of his reign I, Daniel, understood by the books the number of the years specified by the word of the Lord through Jeremiah*

*the prophet, that He would accom-
plish seventy years in the desolations of Jerusalem* (Daniel 9:2).

Even in Babylon, Daniel studied
the Scriptures and discerned God's plan.
Learning anchors us in truth.

Wisdom requires discipline in learning—not just the Bible on our phones surrounded by distractions, but intentional
time in God's Word and in books that build
our faith.

3. Seek Wisdom Through Meditation

The third pathway is **meditation**.
Meditation is the incubation of truth until it
grows into fruit. When we discover a truth
in Scripture, it begins as a seed. Meditation
nurtures that seed until it becomes a tree.

The psalmist wrote: *"But his delight is
in the law of the Lord, and in His law he
meditates day and night"* (Psalm 1:2).

Psalm 119:97 adds: *"Oh, how I love
Your law! It is my meditation all the day."*
Meditation takes truth deeper than hear-
ing or reading. It saturates the heart and
mind until it transforms the way we think.
Proverbs describes the fruit of this process:

*"My son, keep your father's com-
mand, and do not forsake the law
of your mother. Bind them con-
tinually upon your heart; tie them*

around your neck. When you roam, they will lead you; when you sleep, they will keep you; and when you awake, they will speak with you" (Proverbs 6:20-22).

Joshua 1:8 offers the formula for success:

"This Book of the Law shall not depart from your mouth, but you shall meditate in it day and night, that you may observe to do according to all that is written in it. For then you will make your way prosperous, and then you will have good success."

Moses spent 80 years in preparation before God called him to lead Israel. His breakthrough came only after decades of silent incubation. In the same way, as we meditate on God's truth, He prepares us for the moment when our obedience will make an eternal impact.

4. Seek Wisdom Through The Fear Of The Lord

The fourth and most foundational pathway is **the fear of the Lord**. Scripture is clear:

"The fear of the Lord is the beginning of wisdom, and knowledge of the Holy One is understanding" (Proverbs 9:10).

*"The fear of the Lord is the begin-
ning of wisdom; all who follow His
precepts have good understanding"* (Psalm 111:10).

*"And to man He said, 'Behold, the
fear of the Lord, that is wisdom,
and to depart from evil is understanding'"* (Job 28:28).

The fear of the Lord is not terror but
reverence—acknowledging God's holiness,
submitting to His authority, and turning
away from evil. Job was described this way:
*"This man was blameless and upright; he
feared God and shunned evil"* (Job 1:1).

Paul urged believers to live in this posture: *"Therefore, having these promises,
beloved, let us cleanse ourselves from all
filthiness of the flesh and spirit, perfecting
holiness in the fear of God"* (2 Corinthians
7:1). The fear of the Lord separates us from
sin and prepares us to be useful vessels:

*Nevertheless the solid foundation
of God stands, having this seal: "The
Lord knows those who are His,"
and, "Let everyone who names the
name of Christ depart from iniquity." . . . If anyone cleanses himself
from the latter, he will be a vessel
for honor, sanctified and useful
for the Master, prepared for every
good work"* (2 Timothy 2:19, 21).

Without the fear of the Lord, prayer becomes shallow, learning becomes intellectual pride, and meditation becomes self-centered. With the fear of the Lord, all other pathways flow together into divine wisdom.

SUMMARY OF CHAPTER 9

- Wisdom must be asked for through prayer and God promises to give it generously.

- Wisdom grows through continual learning—in Scripture and in disciplined study.

- Wisdom deepens through meditation—incubating God's truth until it transforms us.

- Wisdom begins with the fear of the Lord—reverence and obedience that anchor all other pursuits.

Scriptures For Study And Reflection

1. **Matthew 7:7-8**
   "Ask, and it will be given to you; seek, and you will find; knock, and it will be opened to you. For everyone who asks receives, and he who seeks finds, and to him who knocks it will be opened."

2. **James 1:5**
   If any of you lacks wisdom, let him ask of

God, who gives to all liberally and without reproach, and it will be given to him.

3. **Colossians 1:9**
   For this reason we also, since the day we heard it, do not cease to pray for you, and to ask that you may be filled with the knowledge of His will in all wisdom and spiritual understanding.

4. **Jeremiah 33:3**
   "Call to Me, and I will answer you, and show you great and mighty things, which you do not know."

5. **Proverbs 1:5**
   A wise man will hear and increase learning, and a man of understanding will attain wise counsel.

6. **2 Timothy 4:13**
   Bring the cloak that I left with Carpus at Troas when you come—and the books, especially the parchments.

7. **Daniel 9:2**
   In the first year of his reign I, Daniel, understood by the books the number of the years specified by the word of the Lord through Jeremiah the prophet, that He would accomplish seventy years in the desolations of Jerusalem.

8. **Psalm 1:2**
   "But his delight is in the law of the Lord, and in His law he meditates day and night."

9. **Psalm 119:97**

   "Oh, how I love Your law! It is my meditation all the day."

10. **Joshua 1:8**

    "This Book of the Law shall not depart from your mouth, but you shall meditate in it day and night, that you may observe to do according to all that is written in it. For then you will make your way prosperous, and then you will have good success."

11. **Proverbs 9:10**

    The fear of the Lord is the beginning of wisdom, and knowledge of the Holy One is understanding.

12. **Psalm 111:10**

    "The fear of the Lord is the beginning of wisdom; all who follow His precepts have good understanding. To him belongs eternal praise."

13. **Job 28:28**

    And to man He said, "Behold, the fear of the Lord, that is wisdom, and to depart from evil is understanding."

14. **2 Corinthians 7:1**

    Therefore, having these promises, beloved, let us cleanse ourselves from all filthiness of the flesh and spirit, perfecting holiness in the fear of God.

15. **2 Timothy 2:19-21**

    Nevertheless the solid foundation of

God stands, having this seal: "The Lord knows those who are His," and, "Let everyone who names the name of Christ depart from iniquity." . . . If anyone cleanses himself from the latter, he will be a vessel for honor, sanctified and useful for the Master, prepared for every good work.

Discussion Questions

1. Why is prayer the first and most essential pathway to divine wisdom?

2. What practical steps can you take to become a lifelong learner in both Scripture and daily life?

3. How can meditation transform truth from head knowledge into heart transformation?

4. What does it mean to fear the Lord in your daily life, and how does that shape your choices?

5. Which of these four pathways—prayer, learning, meditation, fear of the Lord— do you need to strengthen most?

6. How have you seen God's wisdom grow in your life when you applied one of these principles?

CHAPTER 10

WISDOM IN MEEKNESS AND THE FEAR OF THE LORD

Wisdom is more than information; it is how we live before God. Scripture teaches that wisdom has a foundation:

> *"The fear of the Lord is the beginning of wisdom, and knowledge of the Holy One is understanding"* (Proverbs 9:10).

> *And to man He said, "Behold, the fear of the Lord, that is wisdom, and to depart from evil is understanding"* (Job 28:28).

The fear of the Lord is the entry point to wisdom. Without it, we cannot understand God's ways. When we walk in reverence, separating ourselves from sin and devoting ourselves to God, wisdom grows in us. Paul reminded Timothy of this:

> *In a great house there are not only vessels of gold and silver, but also of wood and clay; some are for special purposes and some for common use. Those who cleanse themselves from the latter will be instruments for special purposes, made holy, useful to the Master and prepared to do any good work* (2 Timothy 2:20-21).

And again:

> *Therefore, having these promises, beloved, let us cleanse ourselves from all filthiness of the flesh and spirit, perfecting holiness in the fear of God* (2 Corinthians 7:1).

The fear of the Lord separates us from iniquity and prepares us for usefulness. Psalm 25:14 adds: *"The secret of the Lord is with those who fear Him, and He will show them His covenant."*

Job modeled this life: *"This man was blameless and upright; he feared God and shunned evil"* (Job 1:1). His greatness flowed from reverence, holiness, and trust. Yet wisdom is not only rooted in reverence; it is also expressed in meekness.

What Is Meekness?

Meekness is simply admitting inability, accepting weakness, and recognizing the limits of one's capability. It is not timidity or passivity but a humble acknowledgment that apart from God, we can do nothing. True meekness is strength under control, surrendered to God.

The world resists meekness. Ours is an age of competition, where people measure themselves against one another—men against women, young against old, rich against poor. But Scripture calls us to a different posture: not proving ourselves, but humbling ourselves before the Lord.

Jesus modeled meekness: *"Take my yoke upon you and learn from me, for I am gentle and humble in heart, and you will find rest for your souls"* (Matthew 11:29).

When you have wisdom from above, you function in meekness.

1. David: Meekness That Discerns

David's reign demonstrates meekness guided by divine wisdom.

> *"The meek will he guide in judgment: and the meek will he teach his way"* (Psalm 25:9, KJV).

When Joab attempted to manipulate David through a woman's words, David discerned the truth. His meekness gave him clarity to see beyond appearances. Scripture says this kind of discernment resembles the wisdom of angels.

David's life shows us that meekness is

not weakness. It is the posture that allows God to guide us in judgment and teach us His way.

2. Moses: Meekness That Submits

Moses is described as the meekest man on earth:

> *Now the man Moses was very meek, more than all men who were on the face of the earth* (Numbers 12:3, KJV).

When Miriam and Aaron criticized him for marrying an Ethiopian woman, he did not defend himself. He did not retaliate. He trusted God to judge the matter:

> *"Then Miriam and Aaron spoke against Moses because of the Ethiopian woman whom he had married. . . . So they said, 'Has the Lord indeed spoken only through Moses? Has He not spoken through us also?' And the Lord heard it"* (Numbers 12:1-2).

Meekness does not mean ignoring sin, but it does mean entrusting our reputation to God. Moses' meekness enabled him to lead a difficult people with patience.

3. Wisdom In Creation

Meekness is also expressed in our willingness to learn from what is around us. God teaches eternal truths through His creation.

> *"Wisdom calls aloud outside;*

she raises her voice in the open squares" (Proverbs 1:20).

Solomon observed the natural world and recorded lessons:

He spoke three thousand proverbs, and his songs were one thousand and five. He spoke of trees, from the cedar tree of Lebanon to the hyssop that springs out of the wall; he also spoke of animals, birds, creeping things, and fish. And people of all nations came to hear the wisdom of Solomon (1 Kings 4:32-34).

Proverbs 30 identifies four small but wise creatures:

"There are four things which are little on the earth, but they are exceedingly wise: The ants are a people not strong, yet they prepare their food in the summer; the rock badgers are a feeble folk, yet they make their homes in the crags; the locusts have no king, yet they all advance in ranks; the spider skillfully grasps with its hands, and it is in kings' palaces" (Proverbs 30:24-28).

The ants teach diligence, the rock badgers foresight, the locusts unity, and the spider persistence. Meekness admits we do not know everything and humbly learns from even the lowliest examples.

4. Practical Meekness In Life

Meekness also shapes our daily actions. In Kenya, children were taught to rise and give their seat to the elderly. It was an honor to show respect. But in many places today, such courtesy is fading. Meekness is not just a spiritual quality but a practical one. It shapes how we treat people, how we listen, and how we respond to criticism.

Jesus promised: *"Blessed are the meek, for they shall inherit the earth"* (Matthew 5:5). The meek are not trampled upon; they are entrusted with God's inheritance.

5. Meekness In Purpose

Finally, meekness aligns us with God's purpose. When God created Adam, He placed him in a garden already prepared. Purpose came first; Adam came after.

"The steps of a good man are ordered by the Lord, and He delights in his way" (Psalm 37:23). When people or opportunities appear in our lives at the right time, it is not accident—it is divine order. Meekness helps us recognize God's hand and say, "Not my will, but Yours be done."

Prayer Of Blessing

I pray that the wisdom of God will come upon you. May you access and possess it. May you walk, love, and live in the wisdom of God. May His wisdom impact your generation and the lives around you. I declare in Jesus' name that you are a blessing and that blessings will accompany you everywhere you go. May God's wisdom rest upon you, filling you with His Spirit and equipping you for every good work.

SUMMARY OF CHAPTER 10

- The fear of the Lord is the foundation of wisdom; reverence and holiness prepare us for usefulness.
- Meekness is acknowledging our inability and God's sufficiency.
- David's meekness gave him discernment like the wisdom of angels.
- Moses' meekness enabled him to trust God for vindication.
- Creation itself teaches wisdom to those willing to observe humbly.
- Meekness prepares us for God's purpose and blessing.

Scriptures For Study And Reflection

1. Proverbs 9:10
   "The fear of the Lord is the beginning of wisdom, and knowledge of the Holy One is understanding."
2. Job 28:28
   And to man He said, "Behold, the fear of the Lord, that is wisdom, and to depart from evil is understanding."

3. **2 Timothy 2:20-21**
   In a great house there are not only vessels of gold and silver, but also of wood and clay . . . If anyone cleanses himself from the latter, he will be a vessel for honor, sanctified and useful for the Master, prepared for every good work.

4. **2 Corinthians 7:1**
   Therefore, having these promises, beloved, let us cleanse ourselves from all filthiness of the flesh and spirit, perfecting holiness in the fear of God.

5. **Psalm 25:14**
   "The secret of the Lord is with those who fear Him, and He will show them His covenant."

6. **Job 1:1**
   There was a man in the land of Uz, whose name was Job; and that man was blameless and upright, and one who feared God and shunned evil.

7. **Psalm 25:9**
   "The meek will he guide in judgment: and the meek will he teach his way."

8. **Numbers 12:1-3**
   Then Miriam and Aaron spoke against Moses . . . Now the man Moses was very meek, more than all men who were on the face of the earth.

9. **Proverbs 1:20**
   Wisdom calls aloud outside; she raises her voice in the open squares.

10. **1 Kings 4:32-34**
    He spoke three thousand proverbs, and his songs were one thousand and five . . . and men of all nations came to hear the wisdom of Solomon.

11. **Proverbs 30:24-28**
    There are four things which are little on the earth, but they are exceedingly wise . . .

12. **Matthew 5:5**
    "Blessed are the meek, for they shall inherit the earth."

13. **Psalm 37:23**
    "The steps of a good man are ordered by the Lord, and He delights in his way."

Discussion Questions

1. How does the biblical definition of meekness differ from the world's definition of weakness?

2. Why is the fear of the Lord essential for growing in wisdom?

3. In what ways do David and Moses model meekness in leadership?

4. How can observing creation help us grow in wisdom and meekness?

5. What practical acts of meekness could you adopt in your daily interactions with others?

6. How does meekness prepare you to recognize and fulfill God's purpose for your life?

CHAPTER 11

10 HABITS FOR DAILY LIVING

Wisdom is not just knowledge—it is applied knowledge. It is how we live each day in alignment with God's purpose. Scripture tells us: *"Be very careful, then, how you live—not as unwise but as wise, making the most of every opportunity, because the days are evil"* (Ephesians 5:15-16).

Here are ten habits that will help you put wisdom into action every day.

1. Ask God For Wisdom Daily

Scripture: *"If any of you lacks wisdom, let him ask of God, who gives to all liberally and without reproach, and it will be given to him"* (James 1:5).

Principle: Wisdom is not automatic; it is received. Each day brings new challenges, and we need God's guidance afresh.

Practice: Begin each morning with a simple prayer: "Lord, give me wisdom today in my decisions, my relationships, and my responsibilities."

2. Live With Reverence: Fear The Lord

Scripture: *"The fear of the Lord is the beginning of wisdom, and knowledge of the Holy One is understanding"* (Proverbs 9:10).

Principle: Reverence for God sets the foundation for wise living.

Practice: Pause before decisions and ask: "Will this honor God?" Make holiness and integrity your compass.

3. Stay Rooted In God's Word

Scripture: *"Your word is a lamp to my feet and a light to my path"* (Psalm 119:105).

Principle: Wisdom grows as we meditate on Scripture.

Practice: Read at least one chapter of Proverbs or Psalms daily. Write down one lesson to apply that day.

4. Learn From Life And From Others

Scripture: *"Let the wise listen and add to their learning, and let the discerning get guidance"* (Proverbs 1:5).

Principle: Wisdom requires humility to keep learning from Scripture, mentors, and even mistakes.

Practice: Keep a journal of lessons

learned. Write one takeaway each week from a sermon, book, or conversation.

5. Guard Your Heart And Your Words

Scripture: *"Above all else, guard your heart, for everything you do flows from it"* (Proverbs 4:23).

Principle: Words and attitudes reveal what fills the heart. Wisdom requires discipline of both.

Practice: Before speaking, ask yourself: "Is it true? Is it kind? Is it necessary?"

6. Walk With The Wise

Scripture: *"Walk with the wise and become wise, for a companion of fools suffers harm"* (Proverbs 13:20).

Principle: The company we keep shapes our character.

Practice: Surround yourself with people who inspire faith and integrity. Limit time with those who pull you away from God.

7. Choose Diligence Over Laziness

Scripture: *"The plans of the diligent lead to profit as surely as haste leads to poverty"* (Proverbs 21:5).

Principle: Wisdom is often expressed through hard work and perseverance.

Practice: Write out your top three priorities for the day and complete them before moving on to less important tasks.

8. Practice Meekness And Humility

Scripture: *"Blessed are the meek, for they will inherit the earth"* (Matthew 5:5).

Principle: True wisdom is shown in gentleness and humility, not arrogance.

Practice: Each day, intentionally serve someone else—a kind word, a helping hand, or listening with patience.

9. Use Trials As Training

Scripture: *"Consider it pure joy, my brothers and sisters, whenever you face trials of many kinds, because you know that the testing of your faith produces perseverance"* (James 1:2-3).

Principle: Challenges are classrooms for wisdom if we embrace them with faith.

Practice: When facing difficulties, ask: "What is God teaching me here?" Write it down.

10. Leave A Legacy Of Wisdom

Scripture: *"The righteous lead blameless lives; blessed are their children after them"* (Proverbs 20:7).

Principle: Wisdom is not only for personal benefit but for generations to come.

Practice: Share your faith lessons with your children, grandchildren, or mentees. Pass on what God has taught you.

Final Thought

Wisdom is not an event; it is a lifestyle. By putting these habits into practice daily, you will grow in wisdom from above—wisdom that is pure, peaceable, merciful, and fruitful.

CHAPTER 12
GROUP STUDY GUIDE

This guide is designed for small groups, Bible studies, or individual reflection. Use the questions to go deeper, share insights, and apply the lessons. End each session with prayer, asking God to give wisdom from above.

CHAPTER 1
GOD'S PLAN FOR YOUR LIFE

Questions

1. How does Psalm 139:15-16 change the way you view your life's purpose?

2. What are some ways people ignore or resist God's plan?

3. How can you remain faithful when God's plan unfolds differently than expected?

4. Share a time when you sensed God was guiding your steps.

Prayer

"Lord, thank You that my days are written in Your book. Help me trust Your plan and walk in it daily."

CHAPTER 2
WHOLEHEARTED
DEVOTION TO GOD

Questions

1. What does it mean to serve God with a "whole heart"?

2. What distractions or divided loyalties keep people from fully following Him?

3. How can prayer and Scripture strengthen wholehearted devotion?

4. What step can you take this week to love God with your whole heart?

Prayer

"Lord, remove double-mindedness from me. Give me a single heart of devotion to You."

CHAPTER 3
THE THREE C's OF JEROBOAM

Questions

1. How can "cheapness" in worship undermine true devotion?

2. What role does comfort play in weakening our discipleship?

3. How can convenience shape, or misshape, our commitment to God?

4. Which of the "Three C's" is most tempting for you, and how can you resist it?

Prayer

"Lord, help me resist cheapness, comfort, and convenience so I may serve You with sincerity."

CHAPTER 4
DETERMINATION, LOYALTY, AND DILIGENCE

Questions

1. How did Ruth's loyalty demonstrate determination in faith?

2. What does diligence look like in daily Christian life?

3. Why is faithfulness such an essential mark of discipleship?

4. Where do you most need to grow the practice of determination, diligence, or faithfulness?

Prayer

"Lord, strengthen me to be determined, diligent, and faithful in my walk with You."

CHAPTER 5
FIGHTING SETBACKS

Questions

1. How does Joseph's story encourage you if you feel you started poorly in life?

2. What "surprises" in life have tested your faith?

3. How did rejection affect Joseph, and how did God use it?

4. How does God's presence help us through rejection and trials?

Prayer

"Lord, even when I face setbacks, surprises, and rejection, help me trust that You are with me."

CHAPTER 6
BATTLING LIMITATIONS

Questions

1. What family limitations or criticisms have you experienced?

2. How can occupational or workplace challenges test faith?

3. What spiritual weapons does God give us through His Spirit to face "battlefield limitations"?

4. How does meekness help us respond differently to limitations?

Prayer

"Lord, teach me to rise above family, occupational, and battlefield limitations through Your Spirit."

Chapter 7
Types Of Wisdom

Questions

1. What are differences between earthly, intellectual, devilish, and divine wisdom?

2. How can intellectual wisdom become dangerous without God?

3. Why do people turn to counterfeit spiritual wisdom, and how can we resist it?

4. How does Christ embody the wisdom of God in your life?

Prayer

"Lord, give me wisdom from above—pure, peaceable, gentle, and full of good fruit."

CHAPTER 8
WISE LEADERS

Questions

1. How was wisdom instrumental in elevating Joseph, Solomon, Daniel, and Paul?

2. What does Solomon's prayer for wisdom teach us about priorities?

3. How did Daniel's wisdom distinguish him in a hostile culture?

4. Why did Peter recognize Paul's wisdom as extraordinary?

Prayer

"Lord, help me grow in divine wisdom so I can lead others well and glorify You."

CHAPTER 9
WAYS TO GAIN WISDOM

Questions

1. Why is prayer the first step in gaining wisdom?

2. How does learning (study, reading, listening) deepen wisdom?

3. What role does meditation play in turning truth into transformation?

4. How does the fear of the Lord anchor wisdom in daily life?

Prayer

"Lord, teach me to pray, learn, meditate, and walk in reverence before You each day."

CHAPTER 10
WISDOM IN MEEKNESS
AND THE FEAR OF THE LORD

Questions

1. In what ways does meekness differ from weakness?

2. Why is the fear of the Lord essential for wisdom?

3. What can we learn from David's discernment and Moses' submission?

4. How can observing creation teach us humility and wisdom?

5. What daily practices help us live in meekness before God and others?

Prayer

"Lord, clothe me with meekness and reverence. Teach me to walk humbly before You."

CHAPTER 13

CLOSING PRAYER JOURNAL

MODEL PRAYERS FOR WISDOM AND PURPOSE

1.
PRAYER FOR WISDOM

James 1:5
"If any of you lacks wisdom, let him ask of God, who gives to all liberally and without reproach, and it will be given to him."

Heavenly Father, I come before You acknowledging that I lack wisdom on my own. Too often, I lean on my own understanding and try to solve problems in my strength. But Your Word tells me that if I ask, You will give wisdom generously. So today I ask: fill me with wisdom from above. Give me insight that is pure, peaceable, gentle, and full of good fruit. Let me discern truth from error, and righteousness from deception. Teach me how to apply knowledge in ways that glorify You and bless others. Guard me from pride, and keep me teachable. May Your Spirit guide my decisions, my words, and my steps. In Jesus' name, Amen.

2.
PRAYER FOR MEEKNESS

Matthew 5:5
"Blessed are the meek, for they shall
inherit the earth."

*Lord Jesus, You described Yourself as
gentle and humble in heart. You invite me
to walk in meekness, not as weakness but
as strength surrendered to God. Too often
I want to prove myself, defend myself,
or control outcomes. Teach me instead to
yield to You. Like Moses, help me to be
meek in spirit, trusting You to defend me.
Like David, give me discernment rooted in
humility. Help me listen more, speak with
gentleness, and live in a way that shows
others Your grace. May my life be marked
not by arrogance but by humility and
patience. Let meekness make me strong in
You, guiding me into Your will. Amen.*

3.
PRAYER FOR OVERCOMING SETBACKS

Genesis 39:2
"The Lord was with Joseph, and he was a successful man; and he was in the house of his master the Egyptian."

Faithful God, You were with Joseph in the pit, in Potiphar's house, and in prison. You never abandoned him, even when he was betrayed and rejected. Today, I bring my setbacks to You. Some were caused by others, some by circumstances, and some by my own mistakes. Yet I believe that nothing can separate me from Your love. Use every disappointment to refine me and every trial to strengthen me. Help me not to dwell on where I started or how far I've fallen, but to look forward to where You are taking me. Restore my hope. Remind me that You are with me, even in the darkest places, and that You can turn my trials into triumphs. Amen.

4.

PRAYER FOR FAITHFULNESS

1 Corinthians 4:2
"Moreover it is required in stewards that
one be found faithful."

*Lord, You are faithful in all Your ways.
Your mercies are new every morning,
and Your promises never fail. I confess
that my faithfulness wavers. I grow tired,
distracted, or discouraged. Strengthen
me to be consistent in prayer, diligent in
service, and steadfast in love. Help me to
be faithful in small things, so that I may
be entrusted with greater responsibilities
in Your kingdom. Teach me to show up
when it is inconvenient, to serve when it is
costly, and to persevere when it is difficult.
May I hear You say one day, "Well done,
good and faithful servant." Keep me
faithful to the end. Amen.*

5.
PRAYER FOR LEARNING AND GROWTH

Proverbs 1:5
"A wise man will hear and increase learning, and a man of understanding will attain wise counsel."

Father, thank You for the gift of learning. Thank You for the Scriptures, for teachers, for books, and for mentors who help me grow. Forgive me for times I have been lazy, satisfied with little, or proud in my knowledge. Give me a hunger to learn more of Your Word and Your ways. Help me to be humble, teachable, and attentive to wise counsel. Guard me from the distractions of shallow learning, and give me the discipline to study deeply. May I always be a student of Your Spirit, ready to receive correction and instruction. Increase my learning so that I may walk in wisdom and guide others well. Amen.

6.

PRAYER FOR COURAGE IN LIMITATIONS

2 Corinthians 12:9
"My grace is sufficient for you, for My strength is made perfect in weakness."

Lord, I often feel limited by my background, my abilities, or my circumstances. Family criticism, occupational barriers, and personal weaknesses sometimes discourage me. But I thank You that Your grace is sufficient. Where I am weak, You are strong. Teach me to rise above limitations through faith in You. Give me the courage of David who faced Goliath, the perseverance of Jabez who prayed for blessing, and the resilience of Benjamin who overcame a sorrowful beginning. Show me how to rely not on my strength but on Yours. Let every limitation become a platform for Your power in my life. Amen.

7.
PRAYER FOR THE FEAR OF THE LORD

Job 28:28
"Behold, the fear of the Lord, that is wisdom, and to depart from evil is understanding."

Holy God, You are righteous, mighty, and pure. I acknowledge You as Lord of all. Teach me to walk in the fear of the Lord— not in dread, but in reverence and awe. Help me to shun evil, to resist temptation, and to love righteousness. Let my choices be guided by respect for Your holiness. Reveal to me the secret of Your covenant, as Your Word promises to those who fear You. Make me holy, set apart for Your purposes. May my life reflect the truth that the fear of the Lord is the beginning of wisdom. Amen.

8.
PRAYER FOR WALKING IN GOD'S PURPOSE

Proverbs 3:5-6
"Trust in the Lord with all your heart, and lean not on your own understanding; in all your ways acknowledge Him, and He shall direct your paths."

Lord, thank You that my life is not random. You wrote my days in Your book before one of them came to be. I confess that I often lean on my own understanding and try to direct my own path. Today I surrender again to You. Order my steps. Align my desires with Your will. Give me courage to walk in obedience, even when I don't see the full picture. Protect me from distractions that would pull me off course. Help me to live with focus, faith, and purpose. May my life fulfill the reason You created me. Amen.

CONCLUSION

Walking In God's Wisdom
And Purpose

We began this journey with a simple but profound truth: **God's plan for your life is written in His book.**

> *"My frame was not hidden from you when I was made in the secret place, when I was woven together in the depths of the earth. Your eyes saw my unformed body; all the days ordained for me were written in your book before one of them came to be"* (Psalm 139:15-16).

From before your first breath, God ordained your days. This book has explored what it means to discover, embrace, and live out that plan—and to overcome the hindrances that threaten to block it.

Along the way, we have seen how **wisdom is the key** to navigating life's challenges:

> *"Wisdom is the principal thing; therefore get wisdom. And in all your getting, get understanding"* (Proverbs 4:7, NKJV).

Wisdom is not an optional accessory to faith. It is the foundation, the guiding light, the daily resource we must seek if we are to walk in God's will.

The Hindrances
We Have Confronted

This book has identified and wrestled with nine hindrances that keep believers from God's best:

1. **Complacency** — failing to be responsible with God's blessings.

2. **A divided heart or mind** — trying to serve God while distracted by competing loyalties.

3. **Conscious compromises** — decisions that weaken discipleship.

4. **Weakness of will** — lacking determination, loyalty, diligence, and faithfulness.

5. **Blaming a poor start in life** — using beginnings as excuses instead of entrusting them to God.

6. **Family, physical, or occupational limitations** — allowing circumstances to dictate destiny instead of God's Spirit.

7. **Misunderstanding wisdom** — confusing earthly, intellectual, or devilish wisdom with wisdom from above.

8. **Neglecting the examples of wise leaders** — ignoring biblical models like Joseph, Solomon, Daniel, and Paul.

9. **Failing to apply wisdom in trials** — collapsing in the day of adversity instead of standing firm in God's strength.

Each chapter has called us to confront

these hindrances not with fear, but with faith. The message is clear: **You are not an afterthought. Your life has purpose. And with God's wisdom, you can overcome every obstacle.**

Why The Final
Three Chapters Matter

To ensure that this book does more than inform—that it transforms—I have added three practical chapters at the end. My hope is that they will equip you not just to read about wisdom, but to **practice it, share it, and pray it.**

Chapter 11: Wisdom In Action

This chapter gives you **ten daily habits** for living wisely. They are practical steps: asking God for wisdom, living with reverence, staying rooted in His Word, walking with the wise, practicing meekness, choosing diligence, and more. These are not lofty theories; they are habits anyone can practice. My hope is that you will pick one or two and begin right away. Small, consistent habits produce great fruit over time.

Chapter 12: Group Study Guide

Wisdom grows best in community. Chapter 12 provides questions and prayers for each chapter, making this book usable for small groups, Bible studies, or even personal journaling. My desire is that you won't journey alone but will gather with others, open the Word together, and encourage one another in wisdom. As Proverbs says: "*As iron sharpens iron, so one person sharpens another*" (Proverbs 27:17).

Chapter 13: Closing Prayer Journal

Finally, wisdom must be prayed into our hearts. Chapter 13 contains model prayers for wisdom, meekness, faithfulness, overcoming setbacks, and walking in God's purpose. These are not meant to be recited word-for-word, but to guide you into deeper prayer. They will help you move from knowledge to intimacy with God, who is Himself the source of wisdom.

Together, these three chapters are tools. My hope is that they will **move this book from your shelf into your heart, your home, and your community.**

My Prayer For You

As I close, I want to speak directly to you, the reader.

- May you never again believe that your life is meaningless.

- May you never again allow complacency, divided loyalty, or rejection to define you.

- May you stand in the fear of the Lord, clothed in meekness, walking in faithfulness.

- May you embrace daily habits

of wisdom that will shape your character and destiny.

- May you gather with others to study, reflect, and sharpen one another in God's truth.
- And may your prayers rise like incense before God, filled with humility and faith.

Remember: **Christ Himself is the wisdom of God** (1 Corinthians 1:24). When you have Him, you have all the wisdom you need.

A Final Invitation

If this book has opened your eyes and heart to new truth, I rejoice. But don't stop here. Take the lessons and put them into practice. Use the habits of Chapter 11. Share the questions of Chapter 12. Pray the prayers of Chapter 13. Let these pages move you into a deeper walk with Christ.

You are always invited to the congregation I pastor, Truth Bible Church in Tucson, Arizona. We are also on Facebook and online. And if I can serve you or your church as you grow in your walk with God, please do not hesitate to contact me at:

psthiramm@gmail.com

ABOUT THE AUTHOR

Reverend Hiram Njoroge has been in the ministry for over 30 years and has grown to be an effective teacher of the Word. He has pioneered churches in Kenya and now heads Truth Bible Church, a vibrant church in Tucson, Arizona, USA. He is married to Nancy and together they have three children: Alpha, Immanuel and Zedd. When they moved to the U.S. in 2016, Hiram realized that he could do more than just pulpit ministry which has now led to the writing of this, his second book. He holds a master's degree in ministry from Andersonville Theological Seminary in Camilla, Georgia.

www.ingramcontent.com/pod-product-compliance
Lightning Source LLC
Chambersburg PA
CBHW061828040426
42447CB00012B/2866